Arthur E. Crix Jr.
524 Pine St.
Steelton, PA 17113-1913

The
Elegance of Old Silverplate
and some personalities

The

Elegance of Old Silverplate

and some personalities

by Edmund P. Hogan

Schiffer Publishing Ltd

Box E, Exton, Pennsylvania 19341

Library of Congress Catalog Number: 80—52027
ISBN 0-916838-30-7

Printed in the United States of America

Schiffer Publishing Limited, Box E, Exton, Pa. 19341

Acknowledgements

The author is grateful to International Silver Co., for permission to use the photographs and information from their Historical Library and Collection on which this book is based.

Also to A. Christian Revi, Editor of Spinning Wheel Magazine for his help and understanding.

It would be remiss not to thank Richard Croteau, Director of International Silver Company's Audio-Visual Department for most of the photographs. His beautiful pictures of the silver, a very difficult subject to photograph, enhance the pages of this book.

Edmund P. Hogan
Meriden, Connecticut
October 1980

Table of Contents

Introduction

In America, silverplating by electricity started to develop in a commercial way in the year 1847. It spawned a great new industry.

By the 1880's there were at least forty firms in Connecticut alone, making silverplated products, and Meriden, and surrounding towns, became the center of this industry. Meriden, to this day, is known as "The Silver City."

Important factories were established there, as well as in Hartford, New Haven, Derby, Wallingford, Bridgeport, Bristol, Middletown and Waterbury. In the last half of the 19th century, these factories produced some of the finest examples of the Victorian Silverplate so highly prized by collectors today.

Queen Victoria was one of the greatest rulers in English history. She became Queen of the United Kingdom of Great Britain and Ireland and Empress of India in 1837 and ruled for sixty-three years, until her death in 1901. It was the longest reign of any British Monarch.

The Victorian Era named for her, was a period of great industrial expansion and increasing improvement in the lifestyles of both wealthy and middle-class homes. The English poets and writers of the time, reflected this and reflected, too, a greater awareness of and appreciation for the things of nature.

It was an age of elegance and flamboyancy.

All this spread to America and influenced almost every phase of American life. It affected home furnishings, clothing and architecture and fortunately, there still remain some homes and buildings with those grand turrets and "gingerbread" trim.

In the field of silverplate the trend was not evidenced until about 1870, but when it came it continued unremittingly for a period of twenty years. The designs of all manner of articles drew heavily on nature and are ornamented with flowers, twigs, nuts, birds, bees, butterflies, squirrels, cows, goats, dogs, lizards and fish plus little girls, boys, fairies and cherubs.

Victorian Silverplate is characterized by over-ornamentation and elaborateness and to some it has no appeal. But it was entirely in keeping with the times and has a distinctive charm all its own.

Except at the poverty level there was hardly a home that did not have a card receiver, a dinner caster, a butter dish or an ice pitcher. Victorian silverplated articles are representative of a way of life; an interesting period in American history.

Although this book deals largely with the silverplate of the 19th century the reader will also find chapters on some of the 20th century as well as on pewter and britannia wares and glass.

An especially fine example of raised or embossed chasing. A product of Rogers, Smith & Co., New Haven, Connecticut, 1877.

Hand Chasing

The industrial revolution in America, employing as it did the use of steam power and more sophisticated machinery, brought to an end much of the laborious handwork which typified the work of the early colonial silversmiths.

And while this is true, it is also true that a remarkable amount of handwork was still done on the late Victorian silverplate, particularly in the field of ornamentation.

Silverware catalogs of the 1860's, 70's and 80's describe tea sets, for example as available in plain, engine-turned (sometimes simply called "engine") engraved, satin-engraved and chased.

Engine-turning was a machine process, guided by hand. It used a stylus-like tool which cut lines in patterns and produced an interesting ornamentation. Although it was not a common form of decoration, it is still being used in a limited way, primarily on the backs of brushes and hand mirrors in sterling silver.

Satin-engraved was a very popular decoration and survived well into the first quarter of the Twentieth Century. The "satin" part was achieved through the use of a circular wire brush on a lathe and imparted a frosted or satin finish to the silverplate. Into this, the design was cut or engraved by hand with sharp engraving tools. It was a highly skilled operation whereby the metal was actually cut away and removed. The contrast between the engraving and the satin background made a very attractive type of decoration. Some of the old pieces are stamped B.C. on the bottom which signified "Bright Cut" and referred to the type of engraving.

Some pieces were simply engraved in the same manner, but without the satin finish.

By far the most popular decoration seems to have been chasing and here again it was handwork requiring a long apprenticeship as well as native ability. There were two types of chasing - flat chasing and raised chasing and both were used extensively in silverplate from about 1855 through the early 1900's.

The chasing operation cut away no metal, but through the use of small steel tools and a hammer, incised the design into the surface of the metal. Although some of these tools were bought, many of them were hand made by the chaser himself. The ends of these tiny tools had different shapes to make a certain type of mark when struck with the hammer. There were little, chisel-like shapes which could form a line or a twig or a vine, a shape to form a small leaf with a single tap of the hammer. There were shapes for circles of various sizes, shapes to make a matte finish, shapes for fluting. It was not uncommon for a set of chasing tools to consist of hundreds of different forms.

In flat chasing, the ornamentation is more or less all on the same plane while in raised chasing certain portions of the pattern were embossed from the inside before chasing the outside to give high relief to the finished decoration. Despite the fact that this was all handwork, the fine hand chasing was not excessive in price. The Meriden Britannia

11

Company in a catalog for 1861 offered six pieces in the Charter Oak pattern - consisting of Coffee, Tea, Water, Sugar, Cream and Slop for thirty-three dollars Plain and only thirty-nine dollars Chased.

In 1886 a similar service was offered at fifty-two dollars Plain and sixty-two dollars Chased.

In order to preserve the shape of the piece and achieve sharp, clear-cut work any hollow piece was first filled with hot pitch which hardened when cold. This was then melted and cleaned out with solvents - after the chasing was finished. Flat pieces were embedded in pitch.

The art of hand chasing is fast becoming a lost art. A shortage of interested apprentices, plus the relatively high cost of finished pieces will probably end this beautiful type of decoration before many more years have passed.

Satin engraved mustache cup and saucer made by Wilcox Silver Plate Co. in 1895. Marked B. C. for Bright Cut.

Engraver's tools with engraved silverplated cup.

Chasing tools, greatly enlarged, showing a few of the many shapes.

A set of tools used in hand chasing with the chaser's hammer. Tools varied in size, but averaged about 4½" long.

Hand engraved tea set made by the Meriden Silver Plate Co. about 1896.

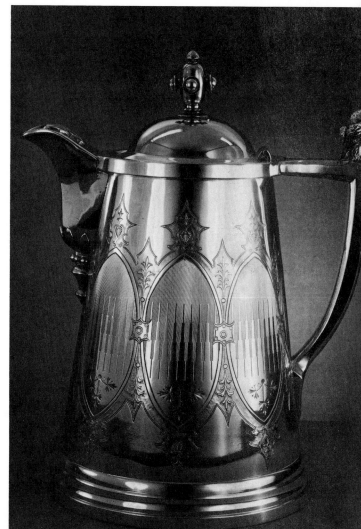

An example of flat chasing. Ice pitcher with porcelain lining made by the Meriden Britannia Co., 1868.

Handsome teapot with engine-turned orna-mentation made by Meriden Britannia Co. in 1867.

Raised chasing has been used on this "Charter Oak" coffee pot made by the Meriden Britannia Co. in 1861.

The Meriden Britannia Company's booth at the Philadelphia Centennial Exhibition. "The Buffalo Hunt" is featured in the front, center, surrounded on either side by cases filled with monumental pieces of silverplate.

16

Sculpture for the Fairs

The Worlds Fairs of long ago had a much greater significance for industry than those of recent years. Before the advent of wide-spread publicity and nation-wide, large circulation magazine and television advertising, they gave manufacturers the opportunity to display their wares to huge audiences of interested and enthusiastic people.

These expositions, as they were called, enabled manufacturers to exhibit their newest designs, and served to introduce to the public new inventions such as the telephone, telegraph, wireless, phonograph, and the automobile.

The first modern exposition, or Worlds Fair, was the Crystal Palace Exposition of London, planned and promoted by Prince Albert, husband of Queen Victoria. This was an enormous "greenhouse" of glass, covering fifteen acres in London's Hyde Park, and it opened May 1, 1851 with seventeen thousand participants.

It was a huge success - so much so that New York City immediately organized a Crystal Palace Fair of its own, which opened in 1853. This was patterned after the London Exposition, but due to a badly leaking roof and subsequent closing and re-opening, never achieved the success of its London counterpart.

The next important fair in this country was the Philadelphia Centennial, which opened in 1876 to celebrate the one-hundredth Anniversary of American Independence. The vast main building was one thousand, eight hundred and eighty feet long, and in the one hundred and fifty-nine days of the duration of the Fair, drew over eight million visitors, which was a record up to that time.

It was the custom of silver makers to create a special display piece for these expositions to demonstrate their skill and craftsmanship, and to serve as a center of attraction for their entire exhibit.

The Gorham Manufacturing Company of Providence, Rhode Island, created the Century Vase, a large display piece including sculptured figures, and measuring five feet four inches long and four feet two inches high. It contained two thousand ounces of solid silver, and was valued at that time at twenty-five thousand dollars.

Reed and Barton of Taunton, Massachusetts, another large silver maker, displayed a Progress Vase which depicted the advance of civilization.

Simpson, Hall, Miller and Company of Wallingford, Connecticut, produced a special multi-faceted water cooler, holding twenty gallons. After the Fair ended, this piece was moved to Hartford, Connecticut, and now rests on a marble top table in the hall of the Connecticut House of Representatives in the State Capitol Building.

The Buffalo Hunt

The Meriden Britannia Company, produced The Buffalo Hunt - a handsome piece of statuary, originally cast in bronze.

Henry Hirschfield, then head designer for the Meriden Britannia Company, engaged the services of one Theodore Baur to create an outstanding display piece for their exhibit. Little is known of Baur, except that he was a German born modeler-sculptor.

The vast herds of buffalo which ranged the western plains had not yet been slaughtered to near extinction in the 1870's, and "Buffalo Bill" Cody, army scout, Indian fighter, superb horseman, marksman and buffalo hunter, was much in the public eye. It was decided to do something to symbolize this phase of the American scene.

Baur opened a studio in Washington Square, New York City, and spent many hours studying the captive buffalo in the New York Zoo, and the American Indian in museums. The result was The Buffalo Hunt, shown in the illustration. It measures twenty-seven inches long, fifteen inches wide, and twenty-two inches high.

After the Philadelphia Centennial, The Buffalo Hunt was widely traveled, being shown at the International Cotton Exposition in Atlanta in 1881; The International Exposition in Paris in 1889; the Trans-Mississippi and International Exposition at Omaha in 1898, and other large fairs of this kind.

In 1882, and again in 1886, it was made a standard catalog item, and priced at three hundred and fifteen dollars in "old silver" finish, and three hundred and twenty-five dollars in "gold inlaid" wherein the Indian's body was plated in red gold, the buckskin breeches in yellow gold, the buffalo bronze color, and the remainder in "old silver." It was also made in a small size, measuring nine and one-half inches high at twenty-three dollars and fifty cents; and the buffalo alone as a paper weight, four and one-half inches high, at five dollars and fifty cents.

There are several known examples of this beautiful action group, one of which is now part of the International Silver Company historical collection, and on display in the showrooms at Meriden, Connecticut.

"The Buffalo Hunt," made especially for the Philadelphia Centennial.

Buffalo paperweight modelled after one used in "The Buffalo Hunt."

Top: Front and back of bronze medal awarded to Meriden Britannia Co. at the Philadelphia Centennial Exhibition in 1876. Diameter 3".

Bottom: Bronze medal (front and back) awarded to International Silver Co. for their exhibit at the Panama-Pacific Exposition in 1915. Diameter 2¾".

The Spirit of the West

Backed by the experience gained in past fairs, the Meriden Britannia Company really outdid itself for the Panama-Pacific International Exposition, held in San Francisco in 1915 to celebrate the completion of the Panama Canal.

The silver sculpture for this Exposition was called "The Spirit of the West," and is five feet high, seven feet four inches long, and weighs six hundred and fifty-nine pounds. It is comprised of the metals used in the silver industry, pure silver, pure gold, white metal and nickel silver.

An illustrated folder, distributed at the time, describes the sculpture thusly:

"On the base are etchings symbolic of the changing conditions which accompanied the trans-

"The Spirit of the West," made for the Panama-Pacific Exposition.

formation of the West. The Indian Council and Buffalo Hunt are memories of a bygone day. The Forty-Niners are represented with their prairie schooners eagerly seeking the land of golden promise, and the miners delving for its generous wealth. At either end are the two figures of Commerce, typifying the Transcontinental Railroad industry and ocean shipping with the waters of the Atlantic and Pacific united through the Panama Canal.

"Surmounting the pedestal, upborne by life-like "grizzlies" are images representing the three great sources of western leadership — stock raising, mining, and agriculture — and over all is the spirit of peaceful Victory, which truly belongs to the youth and energy of the conquering West."

The "Spirit of the West" was described in a San Francisco newspaper as "the largest piece of sculptured silver in the world." It was two years in the making and the work of Louis Gudebrod in collaboration with Samuel Stohr and Louis C. Hiller of the International Silver Company design staff. Stohr designed many attractive patterns, including the popular *VINTAGE* in 1847 Rogers Bros. Silverplate.

Louis Gudebrod was born in Middletown, Connecticut, September 20, 1872, but moved to Meriden, Connecticut with his family at age fourteen.

Later, while working in New York City, he happened into a sculptor's studio which inspired him to become a sculptor, too. He went to Paris and was a student of the famous Saint Gaudens where he worked on many things, including the equestrian statue of General Sherman in Columbus Circle in New York.

Returning to New York, he attended the Art Student's League under Mary Lawrence and Saint Gaudens. In 1901, while still in his twenties, Gudebrod received a silver medal for his Aztecs, which depicted two warriors engaged in tribal rites of sun worship, and made for the South Carolina Interstate and West Indian Exposition.

The year 1904 found Gudebrod with Carl Ritter in Buffalo, New York, where he received a medal for his Lake Huron for the Pan American Exposition in Buffalo. Through this prize, he received a commission to do an eight foot statue of LaSalle for the Saint Louis Exposition in 1904.

There are at least thirty-seven known works of Gudebrod's, including busts, bas reliefs, plaques, small bronzes, etc.

He seems to have been a modest man - avoiding publicity, and was certainly an accomplished one. He died December 6, 1961, in Meriden, Connecticut.

Both Gudebrod and Stohr received medals from the Panama Pacific Exposition for their work on "Spirit of the West."

California Grizzly Bear - six of these supported the central portion of the "Spirit of The West," 8" long, 4½" high.

In 1923, by vote of the board of directors of International Silver Company, this "only-one-of-its-kind" silver sculpture was formally presented to Mr. M.H. deYoung, founder of the M. H. deYoung Memorial Museum in Golden Gate Park, San Francisco.

Some years later, it was placed on long term loan in the "Whitney Museum" near the Cliff House in San Francisco, but has since passed into private hands.

No. 200.　　No. 300.　　No. 400.　　No. 500.　　No. 900.

Call Bells. Meriden Britannia Co., 1861

No. 6300.　　　　No. 6500.　　　　No. 7400.

Call Bells. Meriden Britannia Co., 1878

Call Bells. Reed & Barton, Taunton, Mass., 1885

Call Bells

Both call bells and tea or hand bells seem to have played a notable part in the daily lives of our ancestors. They were used in hotels, boarding houses, banks, schools, sickrooms and homes, and, in fact, in any situation where it was necessary to call an attendant.

In the days when domestic help was both plentiful and cheap, even middle-class homes had maids or cooks, and call bells were used by the lady of the house to signal them in the course of serving meals.

In the last half of the Nineteenth Century, the silverware makers included call bells and hand bells among the great variety of things they were offering to the public and, in fact, combined call bells with other objects they were making such as dinner casters, spoon holders, etc.

The Meriden Britannia Company, founded in 1852, first offered bells in the catalog for 1861. One page was devoted to this showing some eight call bells and three hand bells. These were stated to be "Plated on Bell Metal" (an alloy of tin and copper).

By 1878 some of these styles were continued and new designs added to include sixty-four different patterns in standard call bells, plus eleven "Revolving Bells", three "Patent Strike Bells" and sixteen "Hand Bells" for a total of ninety-four.

The use of fully-modeled figures of children, birds, flowers and animals, which was so characteristic in other articles in Victorian silverplate such as napkin rings, card receivers, etc., extended only to a limited degree in bells. The Meriden Britannia Company showed only three designs of this kind,

in 1878, using a small boy, a cherub and a hand.

But Reed and Barton of Taunton, Massachusetts, illustrated three handsome call bells in 1885 using a bird, a camel and an elephant. They also showed two hand bells with the handles formed of a boy with a baseball bat and a girl with a tennis racquet.

Many of the call bells must have been quite attractive with finishes described as "Old Silver", "Nickel and Verde Base", "Frame Gilt, (goldplated) Black Base" or "Nickel and Blue". Some bases were made of bronze, rosewood and black or white marble.

A very unusual condition is evident in the examination of the old silverware catalogs in that many of the same call bells are offered by six or seven different makers, even to the extent of using identical pictures and style numbers.

For example, in the years from 1867 through 1887 some of the same bells are shown by Meriden Britannia Company, Meriden Silver Plate Company and Wilcox Silver Plate Company of Meriden, Connecticut; the Middletown Plate Company, Middletown, Connecticut; Derby Silver Company, Derby, Connecticut; and Simpson, Hall, Miller and Company of Wallingford, Connecticut.

And it was also true of Reed and Barton of Taunton, Massachusetts, not connected with the others in any way.

While it was not unusual for the silver makers in those days to sell each other certain articles which were then marketed under the buyers' trademark, this was never done to the extreme degree represented by the call bells.

This leads one to speculate that perhaps the silver makers bought bells from bell makers and simply did the plating, assembling, finishing and selling. This may not be too farfetched an assumption since in Meriden, at that time, there were at least two firms making bells - the Bradley and Hubbard Manufacturing Company and the Meriden Bronze Company.

Or, they may have been bought from makers in East Hampton, Connecticut some twenty miles away. East Hampton, known as "Bell Town" is the site of the first bell manufacturer in the United States. William Barton started there in 1808. At one time this small town contained no less than thirty bell-making firms who turned out bells of every description. Of all of these, only one remains - Bevan Brothers Manufacturing Company, under the continuous operation of the Bevan family since 1832.

No. 2400. HOTEL.

No. 4400. HOTEL.

No. 7600. Silver Plated Frame.

No. 7850. Gilt Frame.

Call Bells. Meriden Britannia Co., 1886

24

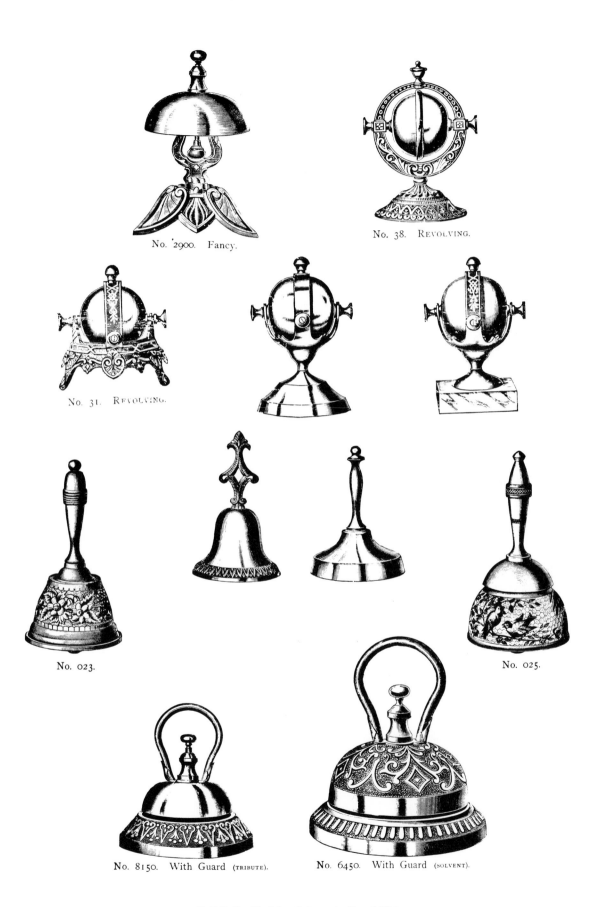

No. 2900. Fancy.

No. 38. Revolving.

No. 31. Revolving.

No. 023.

No. 025.

No. 8150. With Guard (tribute).

No. 6450. With Guard (solvent).

Call Bells. Meriden Britannia Co., 1886

A representative group of figural napkin rings. Left to right; top: Bird, bud vase (5½" high), and Triton, blowing a shell horn (5" high), were made by the Meriden Britannia Co., 1877, 1888, and 1878. Cupids holding napkin ring, by Rogers, Smith & Co., 1878. Center: Kate Greenaway girl with muff (4" high) and boy with dog, made by the Meriden Britannia Co., 1886 and 1878. Pug with glass eyes produced by Wilcox Silver Plate Co., 1884. Pear and leaves, by Barbour Silver Plate Co., 1895. Bottom: Squirrel, made in 1889 by Wm. Rogers Mfg. Co.; bird, by E. G. Webster & Bro., 1873. Bird on wishbone base, Derby Silver Co., 1886. Dog with frightened cat atop ring, by Meriden Britannia Co., ca. 1879. (Except as noted, all pieces illustrated average 2¼ to 3¼ inches in height.)

26

Napkin Rings

The napkin ring (or at least a device to hold a napkin) is reputed to go back to the Fourteenth Century. However, for the purposes of this article, we will deal with the "figural" ring, which many people today collect as an interesting and rewarding hobby.

The trend toward ornamenting napkin rings with fully rounded figures started about 1879 and reached its peak about 1886.

The designers of silverplate of that Victorian period had a closer affinity for nature than we have today. Not only napkin rings, but many other articles in silverplate were ornamented with leaves, flowers, birds, animals, butterflies, etc.

And they were very realistic in their interpretation of these decorations. They took no liberties and made no attempt to "stylize" anything. A goat looks like a goat - a dog like a dog - acorns like acorns - and birds like birds. In fact, they can be looked upon as miniature pieces of sculpture. Indeed, the catalog of 1878 issued by Simpson, Hall, Miller and Company of Wallingford, Connecticut shows an unusual ring representing Rip Van Winkle with the following comment: "This can also be used as a parlor ornament by leaving off the napkin ring."

We can speculate too, that this type of napkin ring may have been a popular gift to children on birthdays and other gift-giving occasions, because so many of the ornaments had "child appeal."

Thus we see the little boy and his dog, a goat pulling a ring on wheels, also rabbits, squirrels, chicks, cats, etc. Some were engraved with the names of the original owners - Simon, Maggie, Robert, and Lynn, for example. A couple of favorites were the little bonneted girl and matching boy - doubtless inspired by the figures of Kate Greenaway. She was an English artist born in London in 1846, and was famous for her illustrations of child life, published in the "Kate Greenaway Birthday Book," and "Under the Window." She died in 1901. These same two figures, without the ring and with holes in the top were offered as individual pepper shakers.

A type of ring which is rare today is the one with the small glass bud vase. The ornamentation on the vase was usually hand enameled.

Although the silver firms of those days were competitors, as they are today, there seems to have been a free and easy exchange among them, and they apparently sold each other various parts or articles which the buyer stamped with his own trademark. So, it is possible to find the same napkin ring (or sometimes just the same ornaments) with two different trademarks.

So popular were these figural rings that in just a three year period - 1886, 1887, and 1888 - five firms in the Meriden, Connecticut area offered eighty-two different designs. These were Meriden Britannia Company, Meriden Silver Plate Company, Wilcox Silver Plate Company, Middletown Plate Company, and Simpson, Hall, Miller and Company, all of which later became part of The International Silver Company.

At the same time, other firms with names like Tufts, Homan, Pairpoint, Derby, etc., were offering extensive assortment, too.

The well known manufacturer, Reed and Barton of Taunton, Massachusetts, in its large 1885 catalog, offered nine solid pages of napkin rings, of which thirty-eight different figural ones were included.

A related piece was what was called a "combination napkin ring," or usually an "individual caster." These varied in size - a simple style, including in addition to the ring, an open salt and a pepper shaker. A more elaborate form added a small bottle for vinegar and a little plate for butter.

By 1900 tastes had changed and the demand for the fancy rings dwindled away to nothing. Despite this relatively short period of about twenty years, hundreds of unusual designs were sold, and new ones turn up in antique shops every day.

GOLD AND SILVER PLATE.

WHITE METAL.

NICKEL SILVER.

No. 250.

Chased,   per dozen, $30.00 (LOBBY).

No. 235.

Chased,   .   per dozen, $24.00 (APPEAL).

No. 251.

Chased,   .   per dozen, $30.00 (L

Kate Greenaway boy and girl, and cat napkin ring, from a Meriden Britannia Co. catalog dated 1886.

Individual casters. Left to right: Wilcox Silver Plate Co., ca. 1873 (ring is ornamented with bird and nest containing three eggs); 5½" high. Meriden Britannia Co., 1873 (little hexagonal plate on rack in back was for butter); 8" high. Simpson, Hall, Miller & Co., 1879 (pepper shaker sits in holder in back of figure's head); height, 6".

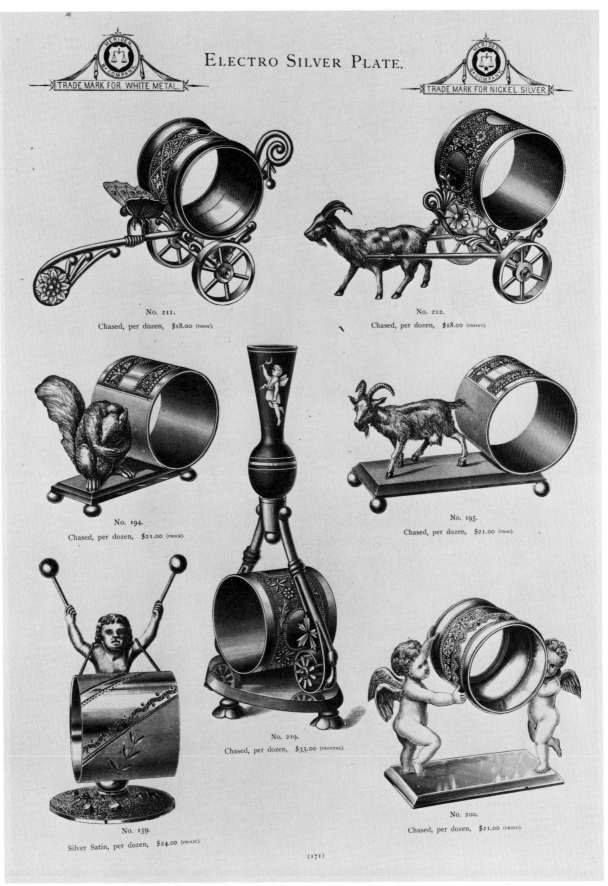

TRADE MARK FOR WHITE METAL.

TRADE MARK FOR NICKEL SILVER.

No. 211.

Chased, per dozen, $18.00 (FRISK).

No. 212.

Chased, per dozen, $18.00 (FRISKY).

No. 194.

Chased, per dozen, $21.00 (FROCK).

No. 195.

Chased, per dozen, $21.00 (FROG).

No. 219.

Chased, per dozen, $33.00 (FRONTAL).

No. 159.

Silver Satin, per dozen, $24.00 (FROLIC).

No. 200.

Chased, per dozen, $21.00 (FROND).

(171)

Figural napkin rings illustrated in Meriden
Britannia Co. catalog dated 1882.

No. 222.

Chased, ... $21.00 (FREQUENT).
Chased, Gold Lined, . . . 24.00 (FRESCO).
Chased, Gold Inlaid and Gold Lined, 27.00 (FRESH).

PER DOZEN.

No. 213.

Chased, per dozen, . . . $15.00 (FRESHET).
Chased, Gold Lined, per dozen, 18.00 (FRESHMAN).

No. 214.

Chased, per dozen, . . . $18.00 (FRETWORK).
Chased, Gold Lined, per dozen, 21.00 (FRIAR).

No. 223.

Chased, ... $39.00 (FRILL).
Chased, Gold Lined, . . . 42.00 (FRINGED).
Chased, Gold Inlaid and Gold Lined, 45.00 (FRIGID).

PER DOZEN.

No. 168.

Chased, per dozen, $16.00 (FRIGATE).

No. 193.

Chased, per dozen, $18.00 (FRINGE).

(170)

31

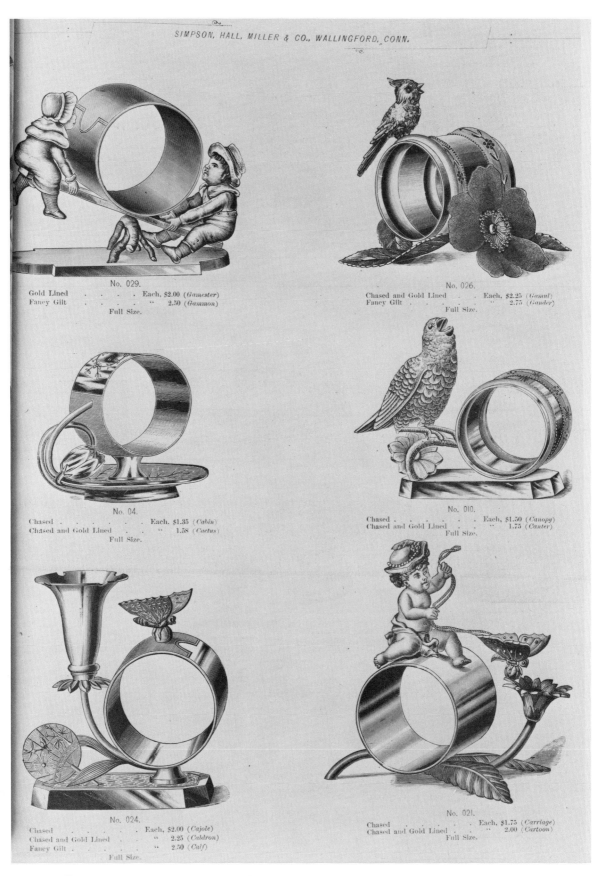

No. 029.
Gold Lined . . . . . . Each, $2.00 (*Gamester*)
Fancy Gilt . . . . . . " 2.50 (*Gammon*)
Full Size.

No. 026.
Chased and Gold Lined . . Each, $2.25 (*Gamut*)
Fancy Gilt . . . . . . " 2.75 (*Gander*)
Full Size.

No. 04.
Chased . . . . . . Each, $1.35 (*Cabin*)
Chased and Gold Lined . . " 1.58 (*Cactus*)
Full Size.

No. 010.
Chased . . . . . . Each, $1.50 (*Canopy*)
Chased and Gold Lined . . " 1.75 (*Canter*)
Full Size.

No. 024.
Chased . . . . . . Each, $2.00 (*Cajole*)
Chased and Gold Lined . . " 2.25 (*Caldron*)
Fancy Gilt . . . . . . " 2.50 (*Calf*)
Full Size.

No. 021.
Chased . . . . . . Each, $1.75 (*Carriage*)
Chased and Gold Lined . . " 2.00 (*Cartoon*)
Full Size.

Figural napkin rings illustrated in Simpson,
Hall, Miller & Co. catalog dated 1886.

32

NAPKIN RINGS.

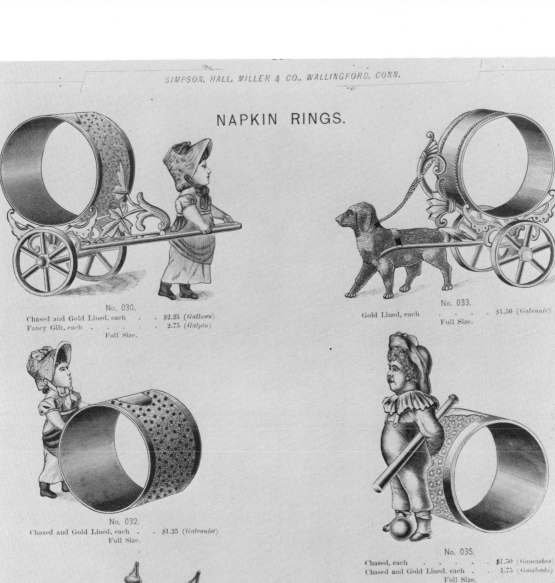

No. 030.

Chased and Gold Lined, each . . . . $2.25 (*Gallows*)
Fancy Gilt, each . . . . . 2.75 (*Galpin*)
Full Size.

No. 033.

Gold Lined, each . . . . . $1.50 (*Galvanic*)
Full Size.

No. 032.

Chased and Gold Lined, each . . . $1.25 (*Galvanist*)
Full Size.

No. 035.

Chased, each . . . . . $1.50 (*Gamashes*)
Chased and Gold Lined, each . . . 1.75 (*Gambado*)
Full Size.

No. 036.

Silver Finish, each . . . . $3.75 (*Gamble*)
Fancy Gilt, each . . . . . 4.50 (*Gambrel*)
Full Size.

No. 031.

Chased . . . . . Each, $1.25 (*Hatchment*)
Chased and Gold Lined . . " 1.50 (*Gameful*)
Fancy Gilt . . . . . " 2.00 (*Gameless*)
Full Size.

No doubt one of the very earliest double wall ice pitchers ever made. A disc soldered on the bottom reads "Stimpson's Patent Double Wall Pitcher. April 17, 1854. No. 4601. Made by Meriden Brit. Co."

It is shown in the very first illustrated catalog issued by the Meriden Britannia Co. in 1855, and priced at $5.00 in britannia (unplated) and at $11.50 in silver plate.

An unusual feature is the hinged flap on the cover which opened when water was poured. Cover is made of a thick solid piece of metal.

Ice Pitchers

Did our ancestors drink more ice water than we do today? Probably not, although the amount of space devoted to and the emphasis placed on ice pitchers in old silverware catalogs might lead one to this conclusion.

In the days before mechanical refrigeration the problem seems to have been, not so much a lack of ice, but some means of restraining it from rapidly melting in the water pitcher.

From Eric Sloane's fine book, *American Yesterday* we learn that the ice business was a major industry in early America. The first ice houses were farm root cellars and by 1830 ice houses were standard equipment on farms. Commercial ice cutting increased and by 1907 there were some 10,000 men cutting ice during the winter months and some ice storage houses were so huge that clouds formed and rain fell within them.

Even in the small town of Meriden, Connecticut, around 1895, population 25,423, the largest of several ice dealers serving the area employed 65 men during the harvesting season and during the summer months used 35 men and 40 horses for delivering ice to homes.

Some indication of the size of the American natural ice business may be gained from Boston figures as early as 1847 which show 51,887 tons shipped to coastal ports and 22,591 tons sent abroad. In terms of dollars this was far above the half million dollar mark and multiplied by the hundreds of other ice businesses it can be seen that it was a major industry.

The invention of James Stimpson of Baltimore of a double wall ice pitcher filled a need and was hailed as a great improvement toward keeping water cool and retarding the rapid melting of the ice.

Patent No. 11819 granted October 17, 1854 (antedated April 17, 1854) was actually issued to James H. Stimpson, his son and executor. Its chief feature was a metal pitcher with an inner body, also of metal, but separated from the exterior by an air space which acted as an insulator against the outside temperature. The patent was extended for seven years and reissued June 9, 1868. It was used on a royalty basis by a number of the silver makers. Some of the ice pitchers turning up in antique shops today have this marking on a metal disc soldered on the bottom.

Then on March 8, 1859 an even greater improvement was patented (No. 23.200) by James H. Stimpson wherein the inner body was porcelain-coated instead of plain metal. This patent was bought from Stimpson's widow in 1868 by H. C. Wilcox acting for the Meriden Britannia Company and the original patent papers and copy of the bill of sale are preserved in International Silver Company's Historical Library.

The Meriden Britannia Co. catalogs of 1871 and 1878 feature these statements:

"The silverplated porcelain lined Ice Pitchers are not only the cheapest and best for service, but are the only pitchers now made that meet the popular demand, there being over forty thousand (40,000) now in use."

Meriden Britannia Co. offered this double wall, metal lined pitcher in 1867. Decorated with a swan finial and large applied medallions on both sides. Height 12 inches.

Porcelain lined double wall pitcher made by Wilcox Silver Plate Co. in 1873. Finial is a frog sitting in a shell and handle a modestly draped female. The chased decoration depicts an eskimo about to spear a walrus or seal. Height 13 inches.

"State Assayer's Office
20 State Street
Boston, June 5, 1868"

"Meriden Britannia Company,
West Meriden, Conn.

Gentlemen: - I have made a careful examination of the PORCELAIN-LINED PITCHERS recently manufactured by you. The lining or inner chamber of these Pitchers is made of WROUGHT IRON, worked into the desired form, and then enameled inside, where it comes in contact with the ice and water. This enamel is a species of Porcelain that has been melted upon and attached to the iron at a high heat; it forms a smooth, glazed surface, like other kinds of Porcelain, AND IS ENTIRELY FREE FROM ANYTHING POISONOUS OR INJURIOUS. These linings have been submitted to a variety of severe tests here, with a view to determine their durability, and power of resisting the corrosive action of natural waters. A quart of acidulated well-water was boiled in one of them without any perceptible action upon the enamel; and, again, a well-water, to which caustic alkali had been added, was afterwards boiled in the same lining, with a similar result. When submitted to sudden changes of temperature, the enamel did not crack or separate from the iron; and sharp strokes with pieces of ice failed to make any impression upon it. If the water in a Pitcher should at any time come in contact with the iron, it would not then be injurious to health. There are many apparent advantages in these linings besides those already mentioned - such as FREEDOM FROM ODOR, AND CLEANLINESS - BUT THE ABSENCE OF ANY INJURIOUS MATERIAL, in the construction of this inner chamber, SHOULD BE THE FIRST CONSIDERATION IN SELECTING A SAFE ICE PITCHER FOR DAILY USE.   S. DANA HAYES,
State Assayer of
Massachusetts

There was a rash of "improvements" in water cooling pitchers for which patents were granted. James H. Stimpson was granted No. 21717, October 5, 1858 for a treble wall pitcher. He acknowledged that this was heavier and more expensive to make but stated that..."for very hot climates and damp atmosphere it is of special use."

"Lyman's Patent Double Valve" issued June 8, 1858 was placed in the throat of the pitcher and kept out the warm air and was used in all those made by Meriden Britannia Company.

Among other patents which were bought by Meriden Britannia Co. was one by Alonzo Hebbard of New York (No. 18546 - Nov. 3, 1857) for "The use of the combination of the woolencloth or felt covering as an elastic non-conducting packing." (around the inner shell.)

One in 1857, No. 190,895 to Edmund A. and his brother, John E. Parker, of West Meriden, Conn. covered construction features whereby the base, outer shell and inner vessel were made separately and joined by bolts between the two walls.

Henry B. Beach (a silverplater at Wilcox Silver Plate Co.) was granted patent No. 8444 (reissue) April 30, 1878 for various construction details which included a metallic covering to be tightly spun over the porcelain or crockery lining to make a stronger lining and "prevent sweating."

Another patent in his name No. 209446, October 5, 1878 included, among other things, a lip or spout so constructed as to prevent water collecting in the spout, getting warm and being shed when the pitcher was next used, (a condition, he stated, was "often to the great annoyance of the person pouring water.")

There was also one for March 26, 1872, No. 124972 to Edmund A. Parker for "the urn constructed with trunnions at its upper edge and suspended in posts, when constructed with the spout and a device thereon for tilting the urn."

Typical of the more elaborately decorated Tilting Pitcher Sets is this handsome one cataloged by Meriden Britannia Co. in 1878. Height 23½ inches.

This small tilting ice pitcher set was probably intended for bedroom use. It was made by Meriden Britannia Co. about 1874.

It is stamped "Patented March 26, 1872" which is, no doubt, Edmund Parker's patent No. 124972 for "the urn constructed with trunnions at its upper edge and suspended in posts." Height 13½ inches.

Wilcox Silver Plate Co. produced this Tilting Pitcher Set about 1885. Drinking cup hangs on a hook at the side. Height 19 inches.

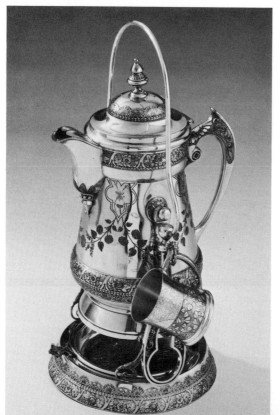

The ice pitchers were heavy, some weighing 10 pounds empty and it was not long before there were a number of inventions patented for stands on which the pitcher could be tilted for pouring. These usually included platforms for one or two goblets and were called "Tilting Pitcher Sets." Some had a cup hanging on a hook on the stand.

Simpson, Hall, Miller & Co. of Wallingford, Conn. in 1868 and again in 1872 featured a "patented corrugated strengthened bottom, applied to all our pitchers." Wilcox Silver Plate Co. in 1886 featured a "removable porcelain lining" and there were others too numerous to mention.

Although there were double, triple, and even quadruple walled pitchers it was the double wall style which survived the longest. However, the Rogers Bros. Mfg. Co. and Rogers, Smith & Co. with which they had an association decided to put their money behind the triple wall style. Both firms, in 1860, published in their catalogs a chart showing the results of a test of various types.

In this test the ice in the triple wall pitcher lasted ten hours before it finally melted and the water temperature stood at 45°. In the double wall it was gone in six hours and at ten hours the water had climbed to 57°.

In a plain "stone china pitcher" the ice lasted only three hours and at the end of the period the water was 72° -- one degree warmer than at the start. During the ten hour period of the test the atmosphere went from 75° to a high of 78°.

Thus was proved the superiority of the triple-wall pitcher.

Some idea of the popularity of the old fashioned ice pitcher may be drawn from the amount of space devoted to them and the variety of designs offered in the old catalogs.

Wilcox Silver Plate Co. in 1868 showed only seven styles offered with a variety of chased ornamentation. By 1886 they showed twelve designs, plus ten tilting pitcher sets.

Middletown Plate Co. showed twenty, plus eight Tilters in 1879 and in the same year Meriden Silver Plate Co. offered sixteen pitchers, eight Tilters and a large ice water urn.

Derby Silver Co. had eighteen pitchers and nine Tilters in 1883.

Meriden Britannia Co., the largest silverware company, started with fourteen styles in 1861–62. By 1867 this had increased to 36; for 1879, 45; for 1882, 46; and in 1886, 35 pitchers, 22 tilting pitcher sets and seven urns ranging from three to ten gallons.

However, by 1896 this had dwindled to fourteen patterns and by 1900 the domestic demand had practically disappeared.

All these firms became part of International Silver Company when it was formed in 1898.

Another large maker of silverplated holloware was Reed & Barton of Taunton, Massachusetts and in a large, handsome catalog issued in 1885 they showed 51 different styles.

The popularity of the double wall pitcher led to other forms, some with outside shells of papier-mache or thick, solid porcelain fitting tightly over the metal body. These were hand painted with colorful decorations in a variety of ways.

Although the domestic demand for ice pitchers faded away around the turn of the century they still continued popular in foreign countries. In a 233-page catalog produced especially for the export trade by International Silver Co. around 1905 or 1906, 29 ice pitchers are shown, plus sixteen tilting pitcher sets.

And where did the warm climate countries get their ice? Why from the ingenious Yankees of course, who had long found it a profitable business. One of the earliest was Frederic Tudor of Boston who in 1805 at the age of 21, borrowed $10,000 and bought the brig, *Favorite*. During December, 1805 and January, 1806 he employed men to cut ice and deliver it to his ship and near the end of February, 1806 set sail for Martinique.

His first voyage was not a success and he claimed to have lost $3,000, largely because the need for and use of ice had not been fully developed.

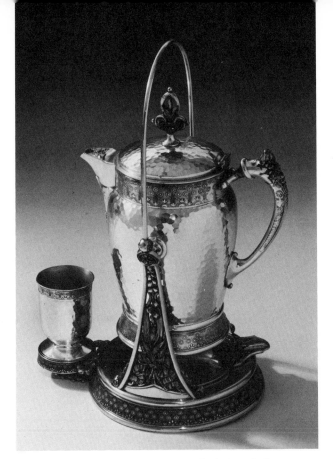

Tilting Pitcher Set in a hammered design by Rogers, Smith & Co. in 1886. Height 18 inches.

Ice urn by Meriden Britannia Co. about 1875. Height 24 inches.

Plated on White Metal.
TREBLE WALL ICE PITCHERS.

The generality with which this remarkable invention is destined to be introduced into use, has induced us to go largely into the manufacture of them, and such is their merit for convenience and economy, that once introduced in a place, they advertise and sell themselves.

Record of an Experiment made with a Treble and Double Ice Pitcher and a Stone China Pitcher, such as are ordinarily used.

At 10 o'clock, A. M., the Pitchers were placed about two feet from each other, on a table, in a room of which the temperature of the atmosphere was 75 deg. Fahrenheit, and $1\frac{1}{2}$ lbs. of Ice were put in each Pitcher. They were examined every hour, by immersing in them the bulb of a thermometer, and the following table shows the time at which the ice melted in each Pitcher, and also the temperature of the water. The Pitcher should be filled with as large pieces of ice as possible, (and then filled with water,) as, in equal weights, a large piece will last longer than several small pieces. It may also be observed, that in a large Pitcher the ice will last longer in proportion than in a smaller one. The Pitcher should be turned on its side when the ice is being put in, so as not to let it fall heavily against the bottom.

Time.	Temperature of Water in Treble Wall Ice Pitcher.	Temperature of Water in Double Wall Ice Pitcher.	Temperature of Water in Stone China Pitcher.	Temp. of Water in Pitcher without ice stand'ng by side of others	Temperature of the Atmosphere.	No. of Hours.
10 A. M.	71 Fahrenheit	71 Fahrenheit	71 Fahrenheit	71 Fahrenheit	75 Fahrenheit	0
11 "	42 "	42 "	46 "	71½ "	.. "	1
12 M.	42 "	42 "	48 "	71½ "	.. "	2
1 P. M.	42 "	43 "	Ice melted.	71½ "	.. "	3
2 "	42 "	44 "	56 Fahrenheit	72 "	76 "	4
3 "	43 "	45 "	60 "	72 "	77 "	5
4 "	43 "	Ice melted.	64 "	72 "	77 "	6
5 "	44 "	46 Fahrenheit	68 "	72 "	77 "	7
6 "	44 "	49 "	70 "	.. "	77 "	8
7 "	45 "	54 "	72 "	.. "	78 "	9
8 "	Ice melted.	57 "	72 "	.. "	76 "	10

Chart showing results of test of the triple wall pitcher versus others as shown in Rogers, Smith & Co. catalog of 1860.

Tudor was delayed in his efforts by embargoes on foreign trade, and the War of 1812 but he was a persistent man and when embargoes were lifted and the war ended he sailed to Havana and built the first successful above-ground ice house.

In 1816 he sold 1200 tons of ice but by 1856 sales had increased to 146,000 tons a year. He shipped ice to Bombay, Calcutta, Havana and even China as well as to southern United States.

On his 65th birthday in 1849 he admitted to friends to being a rich man. He died during the Civil War, in 1864, at the age of eighty.

Other enterprising Yankees followed Tudor's lead and no doubt some of this Yankee ice ended up in the "old fashioned" ice pitchers produced in such great numbers by the Yankee silver makers.

A product of the Derby Silver Co., Derby, Connecticut in the 1880's. Height 13½ inches.

GOLD AND SILVER PLATE.

No. 4941.

Embossed, $8.00 (EMPERIL).

No. 4993.

With Patent Crystal Drainer.

Plain, $8.50 (IRRADIATE).
Embossed, Chased, 9.50 (ISINGLASS).

No. 4992.

With Patent Crystal Drainer.

Plain, $8.50 (INVOLVE).
Embossed, Chased, 9.50 (IODINE).

No. 4940.

With Patent Crystal Drainer.

Plain, $8.00 (EMPLOY).
Chased,   9.00 (EMPORIUM).

No. 4972.

With Patent Crystal Drainer.

Satin, $9.25 (SUBJUGATE).
Chased,   10.25 (EMIGRATE).

No. 4965.

With Patent Crystal Drainer.

Plain, $8.75 (EMOTION).
Chased,   9.50 (EMPALE).

Page from Meriden Britannia Co. 1886 cata-
log shows butter dishes with "sliding" covers.

Butter Dishes

In the "good old days" before butter came in quarter pound sticks, and most people made their own, or bought it from a large tub, an important accessory on the dining table was the silver butter dish. Some of these were sterling, but by far the greater number were silverplate.

As early as 1855, before silverplate had widespread acceptance, the Meriden Britannia Company was offering such dishes in britannia metal (unplated) at fifty-seven dollars a dozen, and the same style silverplated at eight dollars and thirty-seven and one-half cents each.

A little later, butter dishes were also offered in matched tea services. Indeed, for the affluent, a really complete tea service consisted of ten pieces. These were three sizes of pots (for coffee, tea, and hot water), sugar, cream and waste bowl (called a slop bowl), spoon holder, syrup pitcher, butter dish, and coffee urn.

However, it was in the 1880's and 1890's that they had their greatest popularity, and in that period, they were made in great variety, and by all the leading makers of silverplate.

A common feature was the domed cover, necessarily fairly high, to accomodate the butter, which came in a chunk. Usually at the front or the back, there were two little brackets to hold the butter knife.

The manufacturers apparently racked their brains to find ways to take care of the cover when it was removed. Of course some dishes simply had a cover which one took off and placed on the table. Some had hinged covers. On one style, the cover slides up on the two bars which form the overhead handle. Another cover was removable, but had a little hook at the top and a place to hang it on the handle.

A popular style was one called a "revolving butter dish." The dish did not actually revolve, but the cover was fastened at each side with two pins, and by turning a small handle, the cover revolved and passed under the base of the dish. This was considered a great improvement.

Inside of the dish there was a metal plate, or platform, pierced with a pattern of holes for drainage. The butter was placed on this, and pieces of ice put around it. As the ice melted, the water drained into the receptacle below.

In the 1870's, someone came up with the idea of a piece of beveled plate glass to fit over the plate, and with perforations around the frame. This was considered such an improvement that it was patented.

It is described as follows in the 1886 catalog of the Wilcox Silver Plate Company of Meriden, Connecticut:

"Composed of heavy beveled plate glass disk mounted in a strong light metal frame or rim. This drainer is simple, sweet and clean, and cannot possibly give any metalic taste to butter."

On May 15, 1855, James H. Stimpson of Baltimore, Maryland, whose father had previously patented a double-walled ice pitcher was granted a patent on a butter dish which employed the same principle. On the patent papers, he describes it as follows:

"An important advantage of

Left to right: Butter dish from a complete tea service made by the Meriden Britannia Co. in 1896. Butter dish with hinged cover marked Wilcox Silver Plate Co. (ca. 1884). Butter dish with cow finial made by Simpson, Hall, Miller & Co. (ca. 1886).

Left to right: Butter dish with hanging cover, manufactured by Middletown Plate Co. (ca. 1885). Two butter dishes with revolving covers - shown open and partly closed - made by the Meriden Britannia Co. between 1882 and 1887.

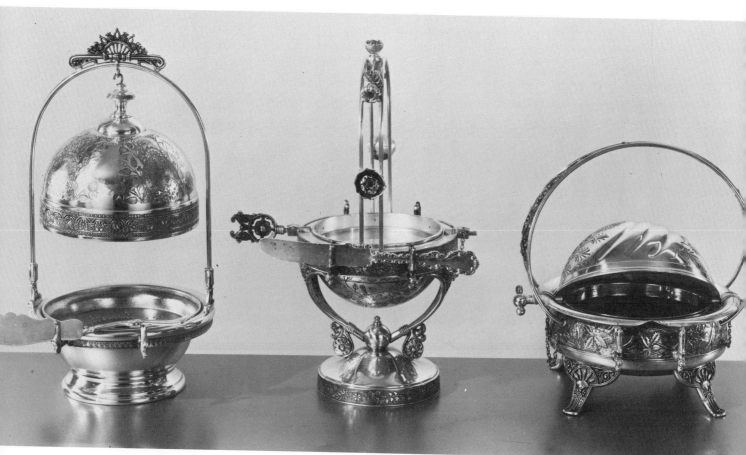

my butter cooler is, the keeping of the butter effectually cool and hard in hot weather, without putting ice on the butter. In the single wall butter cooler the ice is laid on the butter and the water from the ice falls into the dish below. This course is objectionable for several reasons. The butter is injured by the water, the ice is not always clean, and the ice is very much in the way, and very apt to be slipped or pushed out of its place. For these difficulties there is no remedy with the single wall butter cooler, for if the ice should be placed in the dish below, it would melt away with great rapidity, and would fail to keep the butter cool and hard. In short, with the double wall the ice may be placed below the diaphragm or butter shelf, with economy and effect, while with the single wall the ice must be placed upon the butter."

Another patent for a "butter cooler" was granted him July 13, 1858, in which he states:

"The invention consists in having an ice receptacle supported over a butter dish as hereinafter shown, so that the butter will be cooled by the cool air which descends upon it in consequence of being of greater specific gravity than the surrounding atmosphere."

A cow, either standing or lying down was a popular ornament for the cover finial. Almost every manufacturer had his own version of this as a standard design among those he offered.

Illustration from James H. Stimpson's patent for a butter dish, dated May 15, 1855. The butter knife rests on the cow finial.

James H. Stimpson's patent illustration for a butter dish, dated July 13, 1858. In this version the ice is suspended in a container above the butter dish.

Handsome 6 bottle dinner caster with deer head ornaments. Made by the Meriden Britannia Co. between 1855 and 1867. Height 18".

Dinner Casters

One thing fairly common in antique shops today is the silverplated dinner caster. Some people call them "cruet sets", but the true name is dinner caster, according to the old catalogs of silver manufacturers.

That they are relatively common now is an indication of their original popularity, but few people today realize what a huge market existed in years gone by.

They were used extensively in private homes, of course, but found wide use also in public dining rooms and boarding houses.

In a delightful book entitled, *Journey to Day before Yesterday*, the author, E. R. Eastman, tells of his life as a farm boy, and relates a journey taken by horse and wagon to a fairly large town some miles away. A stop was made for dinner at a hotel where he says each dining table was set with a "revolving caster with slots in it for bottles holding, among other things, vinegar, pepper-sauce, and catsup."

Dinner casters were even used on ships, and one catalog dated 1855, shows a caster with the note "with loaded (weighted) bottom for ships."

A representative order for silverware to a manufacturer that did not include 25 or 50 casters was unusual, and many large dealers bought them in lots of 100 to 500.

This popularity was great for the silver makers, of course, but it was important business also for the glass makers, and glass cutters, who supplied the bottles.

There was a glass cutting firm in Meriden, Conn. in the 1880s called Bergen & Niland, who had an extensive line of fine cut glass, but they also furnished cut and engraved caster bottles to the silver makers. It has been recorded, that in one year, 1884, they sold the Meriden Britannia Co. 240,000 bottles. This was enough to equip 48,000 of the standard five bottle casters.

Another firm in Meriden that made caster bottles was the Meriden Flint Glass Co. They were in business from 1876 to 1885, and made bottles as well as cut them.

Dinner casters were a standard item among all the better known silver makers right from the beginning of the electro-plate business. Early styles, particularly during the 1860's, were very attractive, and probably took their inspiration from foreign styles. Even as early as 1861, the Meriden Britannia Co. offered 75 different patterns. There were five or six different designs in the cut glass bottles, and while these were usually simply identified by number, two of them were named --"Jenny Lind" and "Diamond." Good examples of these are hard to find today.

Between 1853 and 1871, there were even toy casters in unplated Britannia ware. They came in four and five bottle styles, with a choice of five patterns in cut glass bottles named "Jenny Lind", "General Taylor", "Ocatgon", "Punty", and "Split and Flute."

In 1860, a most unusual caster was offered by Meriden B. Co. This was called "Green's Patent Vertically Revolving Caster", and it employed the same principle as the Ferris wheel, but was some 33 years ahead of it.

The Ferris wheel, so popular at fairs and carnivals, was the invention of G. W. Gale Ferris, a mechanical engineer of Galesburg, Illinois. He built the first one for the World's Columbian Exposition in Chicago in 1893. This first one was the largest of all. It soared to the incredible height of 268 feet, and had 36 cars, each of which could carry 60 persons. (Present day Ferris wheels are forty to fifty feet high.)

Green's "Ferris wheel type" caster was apparently not a success, because it is not shown again in later catalogs.

It was about 100 years ago that the type we see today came into its own. They were made in four, five, six, and seven bottle styles on a revolving base. Those with five and six bottles seem to have been the most popular. The four bottle style had cruets for oil and vinegar, a shaker for salt, and a mustard jar (no pepper). The five bottle had oil, vinegar, salt, pepper, and mustard. The six and seven bottle designs added extra cruets.

There was also a type called a combination caster, which had a removable bowl-like base which could be used separately as a nut or fruit bowl.

The Meriden Britannia Co. at that time was the largest silverware company in the world. In 1886 they issued a huge dealer catalog, measuring 12″ by 16″ and included 3,200 wood engravings.

It illustrates 72 dinner casters priced from $3.75 to $28.50 with simple bottles. At the same time, they offered a choice of 23 different styles of bottles, ranging from inexpensive engraved styles to the finest heavy cut glass costing $30.00 a dozen. Most of these bottles were crystal, but there were also very handsomely cut bottles in amber, blue and cranberry.

An additional choice could be had in handles -- four styles with flower vases, and six others with call bells.

All the other smaller firms, which later joined together to form International Silver Co., were doing the same thing. Some of these firms were Wilcox S. P. Co., Meriden S. P. Co., Wm. Rogers Mfg. Co., Simpson Hall Miller & Co., and Rogers, Smith & Co.

And there were also such firms as Reed & Barton of Taunton, Mass., Pairpoint Mfg. Co. of New Bedford, Mass., Homan Mfg. Co. of Cincinnati, Ohio, and others, all making as many dinner casters as they could sell. The size of the business on this one item must have been tremendous.

By 1893, the demand started to wane, and the relatively few made in the following years were sold mostly in rural and export markets. They went out of style entirely in the early 1900s.

Casters offered in an 1855 Meriden Britannia Co. catalog.

No. 2590. 6. No. 34 Bottles. Basket.

No. 2580. 6 No. 53 Bottles. Basket.

No. 2540. 6. No. 70 Bottles. Band revolves.

Toy caster made by the Meriden Britannia Co., 1855.

Green's Patent Vertically Revolving Caster made by the Meriden Britannia Co. in 1860. Height 15 inches.

No. 67.

Plain, 5 No. 12 Bottles, . $6.00 (CONCRETE).
Plain, 5 No. 13 Bottles, . 6.50 (CONCUR).

No. 70.

Plain, 5 No. 14 Bottles, . $5.50 (CORBAN).
Chased, 5 No. 14 Bottles, . 6.00 (CORBEL).

No. 76.

Plain, 5 No. 2 Bottles, . $5.00 (BARBECUE).
Chased, 5 No. 2 Bottles, . 5.50 (BARQUE).

No. 64.

Plain, 5 No. 13 Bottles, . $6.75 (CONCEDE).
Chased, . . . Bottles, . 7.25 (CONCISE).

No. 74.

Plain, 5 No. 14½ Bottles, . $5.75 (COLONEL).
Chased, 5 No. 14½ Bottles, . 6.25 (COLONIST).

No. 67.

Chased, 5 No. 12 Bottles, . $6.50 (CONCH).
Chased, 5 No. 13 Bottles, . 7.00 (CONCISE).

*Dinner casters illustrated in an 1886 Meriden
Britannia Co. catalog.*

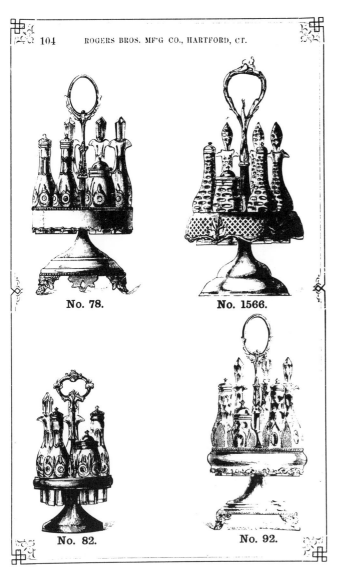

No. 78.

No. 1566.

No. 82.

No. 92.

Dinner casters illustrated in an 1860 Rogers Bros. Mfg. Co. catalog.

Six bottle caster with calla lily handle. Wilcox Silver Plate Co., 1871. Height 17½".

51

DINNER CASTER BOTTLES.

(PRICES PER DOZEN.)

(ONE-THIRD SIZE.)

No. 2, $4.50.   No. 14½, $5.25.   No. 12, $4.50.   No. 14, $4.50.   No. 11, $5.75.   No. 13, $5.25.   No. 16, $8.50.

No. 17, $5.25.   No. 18, $7.00.   No. 19, $7.00.   No. 20, $9.00.   No. 21, $6.00.   No. 22, $5.75.   No. 23, $7.00.   No. 24, $7.50.

No. 96, $15.00.   No. 102, $30.00.   No. 104, $30.00.   No. 95, $18.00.   No. 97, $18.00.   No. 98, $18.00.   No. 99, $20.00.   No. 101, $18.00.

BOTTLES INTERCHANGED IN CASTERS AS FOLLOWS:

CLASS A. Nos. 2, 02½, 12, and 14, Nos. 14½ and 17,	Without extra charge.	Nos. 16 and 20, ... $2 00 per Caster more than Class A.
	$0.25 per Caster more than Class A.	Nos. 96 and 90, ... 3.50 per Caster more than Class A.
Nos. 11, 13, 15, 18, 19, 21, and 22,	.50 per Caster more than Class A.	Nos. 94, 95, 97, 98, 99, and 101, 7.00 per Caster more than Class A.
No. 23. Crystal, ...	.75 per Caster more than Class A.	Nos. 91, 102, 103, and 104, . 12.00 per Caster more than Class A.
Nos. 24, Crystal, and 23, Colored, .	1.00 per Caster more than Class A.	

(99)

*Illustration of dinner caster bottles from an
1886 Meriden Britannia Co. catalog.*

52

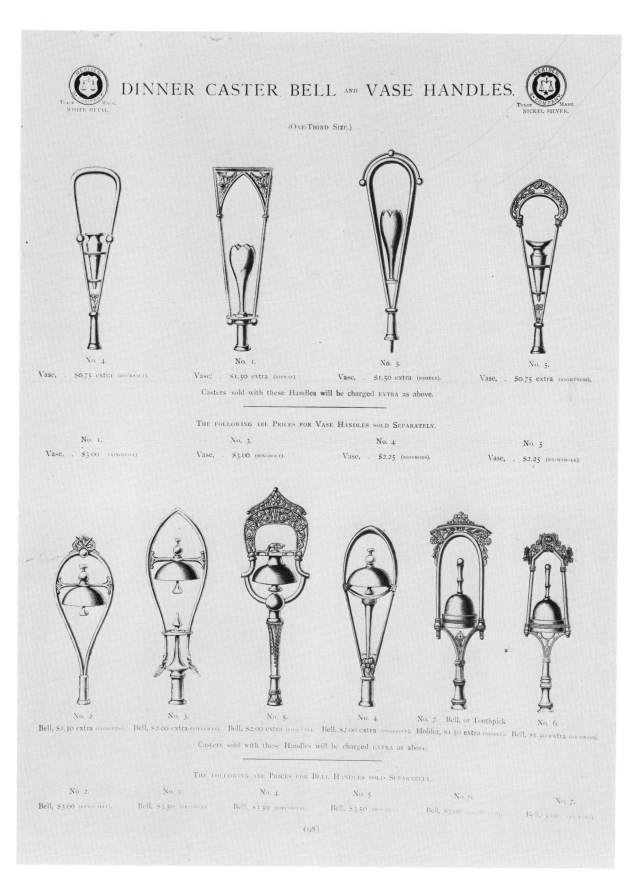

DINNER CASTER BELL AND VASE HANDLES.

(ONE-THIRD SIZE.)

No. 4.

No. 1.

No. 3.

No. 5.

Vase, . $0.75 extra (ROCKSALT).

Vase, . $1.50 extra (RIPRAP).

Vase, . $1.50 extra (RISIBLE).

Vase, . $0.75 extra (RIGHTNESS).

Casters sold with these Handles will be charged EXTRA as above.

THE FOLLOWING ARE PRICES FOR VASE HANDLES SOLD SEPARATELY.

No. 1.

No. 3.

No. 4.

No. 5

Vase, . $3.00 (RINGDOVE).

Vase, . $3.00 (RINGBOLT).

Vase, . $2.25 (RIGOROUS).

Vase, . $2.25 (RIGMAROLE).

No. 2.

No. 3.

No. 5.

No. 4.

No. 7. Bell, or Toothpick

No. 6.

Bell, $1.50 extra (RIGHTNESS). Bell, $2.00 extra (RILEMAN). Bell, $2.00 extra (RIGIDITY). Bell, $2.00 extra (RINGBOLD). Holder, $1.50 extra (RIDDLE). Bell, $1.50 extra (RICHNESS).

Casters sold with these Handles will be charged EXTRA as above.

THE FOLLOWING ARE PRICES FOR BELL HANDLES SOLD SEPARATELY.

No. 2.

No. 3.

No. 4.

No. 5.

No. 6.

No. 7.

Bell, $3.00 (RIDGE ARET). Bell, $3.50 (REVISIONS). Bell, $3.50 (RHYMSTER). Bell, $3.50 (RIGORISM). Bell, $3.00 (RATTLING). Bell, $3.00 (REVILLER).

(98)

Dinner caster bell and vase handles from a
Meriden Britannia Co. catalog, 1886.

53

Early examples of single and double pickle casters. Glass inserts are of cut crystal. Height of double caster 11 inches.

Pickle casters with bail handles and jars of gold decorated ruby glass (left) and gold decorated satinglass (right). Height of tallest caster is 8 inches.

Squat pickle caster in Rose Sunset Glass with Coraline decoration. Height 6 inches.

Pickle Casters

The pickle caster was one of the standard offerings of silverware makers a century ago and ranked equally in popularity with such things as cake baskets, dinner casters, tea sets, ice pitchers and figural napkin rings.

In the old-time grocery and general stores, cucumber pickles were sold in bulk from brine-filled casks but our forebears did a great amount of home-canning, preserving and pickling as well. They pickled a variety of fruits and vegetables besides cucumbers including beans, beets, onions, peppers, green tomatoes, watermelon rind, peaches, apples, pears, plums and grapes, and they served them all in style in the pickle caster.

Beginning about 1882, the glass jars seem to have settled into a pattern of straight-sided round forms which were produced in a tremendous variety of colors, patterns and decorations, and although these were highly attractive, the jars used in 1880 and all through the 1870's show more imagination in the shapes and the decorations.

The glass used was both domestic and imported and in crystal, ruby, blue, topaz, amethyst and other colors. Decorations were in various colors and in gold.

One jar is called "Rubena Glass" and another "Rose Sunset Glass" on which the decoration is very similar to that known as Coraline.

Some pickle casters simply consisted of the jar with a silverplated rim, cover and handle but the more elaborate styles had fancy footed frames which were frequently decorated with cherubs, butterflies, deer heads, cucumbers, strawberries and applied medallions.

The stand usually included a hook or rack for the serving piece which could be a long handled pickle fork, a pickle fork with cutting tine or, most commonly, pickle tongs. These tongs, at the time, ended in the shape of a woman's hand (with a ring on the forefinger).

Prices ranged anywhere from four dollars and twenty-five cents to eight dollars for the single styles and from nine dollars to fifteen dollars for the double pickle casters.

The accompanying illustrations show pickle casters made by Wilcox Silver Plate Company of Meriden, Connecticut from about 1871 to 1882.

Pickle caster with ruby glass jars; the jar on the right has been Coraline decorated. Height of tallest caster is 12 inches.

Pickle Casters.

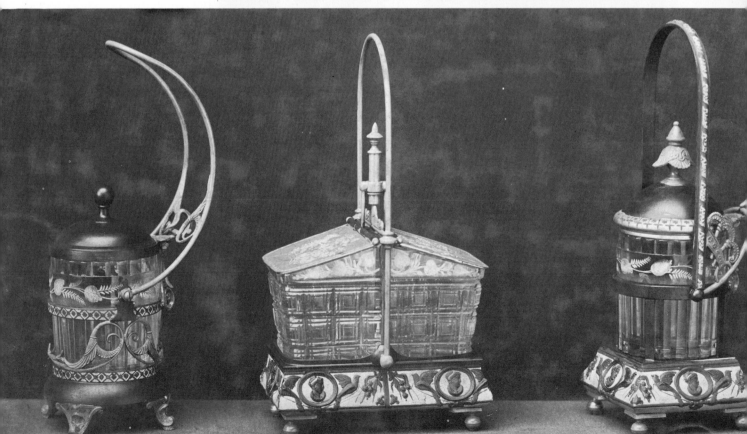

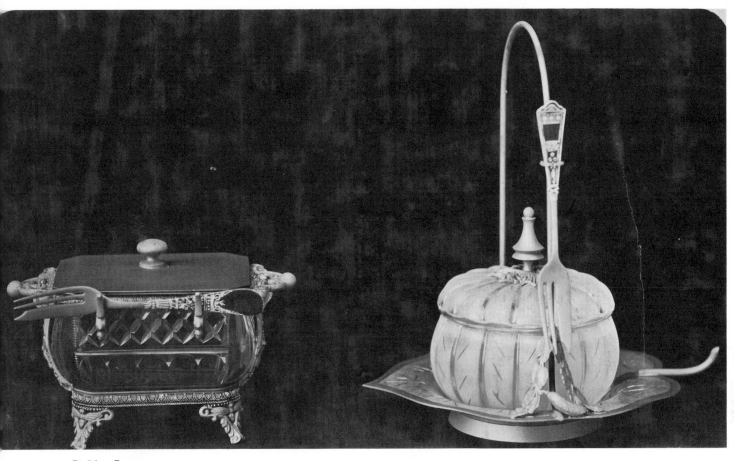

Pickle Casters.

Cracker or Biscuit Jars

Many products were offered by silverware makers in the Victorian period and among them the cracker or biscuit jars must be regarded as one of the most attractive.

They became popular in England about 1865, by which time England had monopolized the tea trade, and serving tea became a national tradition which has survived through all the years.

The cracker jar often accompanied the tea service and became a handsome decoration on the dining room sideboard.

In America, silverware makers did not offer them to any great extent until the 1880's, but in the years following they were cataloged by practically all the leading makers. Some jars were made entirely in silverplate but by far the greater number used ceramic pottery or glass, mounted with a rim, cover and handle in silverplate. More elaborate styles used a complete footed frame.

Types of jars included those of pottery, porcelain, stoneware, earthenware, mould blown and pressed glass, cased glass, opal and satin glass, in every conceivable color, clear glass and beautifully cut glass. And all, except the cut glass, were highly decorated in tasteful colors and designs.

American silverware makers imported many of these jars from England and Europe but also bought from domestic makers as well. From 1876 to 1885 the Meriden Flint Glass Co. was a supplier for most of the local companies.

As was true in numerous other cases, where glass was part of the final product, the silverware makers gave only meager descriptions of the glass itself. They were satisfied in most cases to say such things as "Blue Jar, richly decorated" or "Decorated in Blue and Gold".

The Middletown Plate Co. was somewhat more specific with descriptions like "Blue Agate, Spiral Decoration", "Blue and Rose Agate Spiral Decoration", "Rose Satin Porcelain", and "Rose Porcelain". The Forbes Silver Co. offered one in "Delft Ware".

The accompanying illustrations show cracker or biscuit jars cataloged by the Wilcox Silver Plate Co. of Meriden, Connecticut, and the Middletown Plate Co. of Middletown, Connecticut, both about 1880.

Wilcox Silver Plate Co. was organized in 1865 as Wilcox Britannia Co., but changed the firm name two years later. Middletown Plate Co. was formed in 1864 and both these companies became part of International Silver Co. in 1898.

Trademarks of the silver companies can usually be found inside the cover or on the rim holding it. On the jars with footed frames the mark is on the underside of the frame or on one of the feet.

A collection of cracker jars makes an impressive and handsome display and collecting them can become a satisfying and rewarding hobby.

Biscuit Jars

60

61

*Out of character, but typical of the period,
is the figure of a winged fairy seated on a crescent
moon atop this shell-shaped fruit and nut bowl with
coral-shaped feet. Middletown Plate Co., ca. 1888.
Height 11½ inches.*

Nut and Fruit Bowls

If we can judge from a study of the silverware catalogs of long ago, nuts and fruit of all kinds played an important part in the meals during the last quarter of the Nineteenth Century, not only in homes but also in the menus of some of the finest hotels in the country which frequently ended full course dinners with "assorted nuts and fruit."

Perhaps not more so than today, but at least the serving and eating utensils for these foods had more style.

Many readers, among the older generation, can no doubt recall the fun of nutting trips in the fall and the gathering of shagbark hickory nuts, black walnuts, butternuts and hazel nuts which were much more abundant than they are today. There was also the native chestnut before the blight in the early 1900's eliminated that variety from our fields and woods, the California walnut and imported nuts such as Brazil nuts.

These had to be cracked and picked out and the manufacturers of silverplate, as they did in so many other cases, catered to this need.

Founded in 1852, the Meriden Britannia Company cataloged nut cracks in 1878 and nut picks in nine different patterns as early as 1875.

Although nut bowls were never offered in as great a variety of designs as other popular pieces like dinner casters, pickle casters, butter dishes, etc. there was hardly a catalog of leading makers issued between 1877 and 1893 that did not show at least two or three.

Frequently these bowls were made to resemble nut shells. (One by Middletown

Plate Company is in the shape of a sea shell.) Just as the cow was a favorite ornament or finial on butter dishes of that period, and a small fish on sardine boxes so was the figure of a squirrel most often used on nut bowls. Some of these little figures had glass eyes. Of course, after about 1900, bowls of many kinds continued to be made but they were not specifically called nut bowls and were more restrained in design. Gone were the squirrels, odd shapes and over-ornamentation which was characteristic during the 1870's and '80's.

The various silverplated bowls, baskets and stands for holding fruit date back earlier than nut bowls and were made in much greater variety and over a longer period of time (at least by the many predecessors of International Silver Company.)

For example, Meriden Britannia Company priced two designs in the 1855 price list. The Rogers Brothers Manufacturing Company (1853) showed four designs in 1854. In the earliest years these were entirely in silverplate, later had attractive glass bowls in cut or pressed glass and still later the highly decorated, ruffled and colorful art glass in what we now call "Brides Baskets."

Apparently it was the custom to cut and peel the apples, pears and peaches served at table and individual fruit knives were popular. They were made with several different shaped blades and frequently like the nut cracks silverplated on steel.

One of the most popular patterns seems to have been one called "Arabesque." It was an "all-over" pattern, achieved through

Nut bowl made in the shape of a walnut shell and decorated with applied pears and leaves was made by the Wilcox Silver Plate Co. in 1886. Height 9 inches.

The squirrel sitting on the rim of this silver-plated nut bowl has glass eyes. Made by the Derby Silver Co., Derby, Connecticut, about 1890. Height 6¾ inches.

Branches, leaves and berries, and a tiny squirrel decorate this handsomely chased nut bowl made by the Wilcox Silver Plate Co. in 1880. Height 10 inches.

Illustrated in Simpson, Hall, Miller & Co.'s 1887 catalog as their "Venetian Nut Bowl," this one is embellished with full relief figures of a dragonfly, a bee, and hazel nuts. Originally, this model was made with the ornaments and handle gold-plated (called "gold inlaid"), the remainder of the piece finished in "old silver." Height 9½ inches.

Oak leaves and a tiny squirrel decorate this footed nut bowl made by Wm. Rogers Mfg. Co. of Hartford, Connecticut, in 1886. Height 7½ inches.

etching so the design continues around the sides of the handles as well as the front and back. It was made in a variety of motifs, fruit, flowers, scrolls, etc. and continued in popularity from about 1886 to 1912.

In a highly informative and useful book by Noel D. Turner entitled *"American Silver Flatware 1837–1910"* (A. S. Barnes and Company, Inc., Cranbury, New Jersey) the author quotes from *"Decorum: A Practical Treatise on Etiquette"* by an anonymous "Lady of Fashion" published in 1878. "An apple, pear or peach should be peeled with a silver knife, and all fruit should be broken or cut. Never pare an apple or a pear for a lady unless she desires you and then be careful to use your fork to hold it."

That nuts and fruits were related, as food commonly served, may be surmised from the small folding pocket fruit knives some of which contained a blade for cutting and peeling and also a nut pick. Also offered at that time were boxed sets consisting of six individual fruit knives and six nut picks.

Fruit knives remained in demand well into the present century. They were made in both the hollow handle and solid handle styles in 1847 Rogers Bros. patterns now popular with collectors such as *VINTAGE* introduced in 1904, *CHARTER OAK* in 1906 and many other patterns as late as the 1930's. These later styles, however, had longer blades and were sometimes made with a "saw-back."

Left: Pocket fruit knife with nut pick made by Wm. Rogers Mfg. Co., Hartford, Connecticut, in 1888. Length 5½". Right: Pocket fruit knife without a pick made by the Meriden Britannia Co. in 1867; engraved "Jennie" on the reverse side. Length 5½ inches.

Fruit knives silverplated on steel by the Meriden Britannia Co. in 1887.

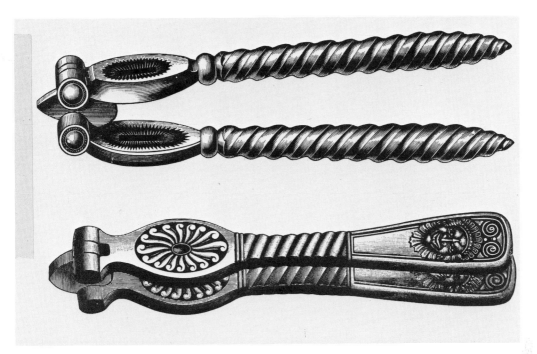

Nut-Cracks shown in a Meriden Britannia Co. catalog dated 1887.

Set of six fruit knives and nut picks made by Wm. Rogers Mfg. Co. ca. 1890. Box is covered with blue velvet and satin lined.

Fig. 1. A handsome coffee urn marked "Rogers Bros. Mfg. Co." This mark was used by them when they were located in Hartford, Conn., 1853–1862. Height 18 inches.

Fig. 2. Teapot made by Rogers Bros. Mfg. Co., ca. 1857. Height 10 inches.

Fig. 3. A classical Greek Key border was used on this teapot made by the Rogers Bros. Mfg. Co., about 1855. Height 10½ inches.

Fig. 4. A decoration called "Engine Turning" was used on this fine teapot marked "Meriden Brita' Co." This was an early form of a mark used by the Meriden Britannia Co. of Meriden, Conn. The pot was shown in their 1867 catalog. Height 11".

Tea Sets

Comparatively few of the many types of articles made in Nineteenth Century silverplate have survived the enormous changes in the dining habits and general way of life which have taken place in the last one hundred years.

Such things as pickle casters, dinner casters, fancy napkin rings, domed butter dishes, toilet-stands, card receivers, and ice pitchers, to name only a few, which were found in almost any home in the old days, have no place at all in the homes of today.

There is one notable exception however, and that is the tea and coffee service. Through all the years, in pewter, coin silver, sterling, and silverplate, there has been a steady procession of teaware.

For this reason, it is possible and interesting to observe the changes in design which have occurred, particularly the amazing change in that period we now call Victorian.

Complete tea services were not made in pewter, although many tea and coffee pots were, and the early coin silver and sterling sets were usually custom made.

In this chapter we confine ourselves to silverplate, beginning about 1855. The tea pots and coffee pots, and coffee urns, at that time were quite handsome, perhaps because they were copied from, or at least took their inspiration from, classic designs from the Old World.

Two fine examples are the coffee urn (Figure 1) made by the famous Rogers Brothers of Hartford, Connecticut ca. 1857 and the tea pot (Figure 2) made by them around the same time.

They also made the attractive plain style with a simple Grecian Key border shown in Figure 3 about 1855.

A somewhat more ornate style (Figure 4) is this one offered by the Meriden Britannia Company in their catalog for 1867 The decoration is called "engine turned."

Most of the standard tea and coffee services of the 70's and 80's consisted of six pieces, including three pots. The largest of these was the coffee which, in addition to the trademark and style number, was sometimes stamped 7. The tea pot was stamped 6, the third pot for hot water, stamped 5. This was the capacity in half-pints.

In addition many sets had a matching coffee urn, spoonholder, butter dish, and syrup pitcher.

For simplicity, illustrations are of the coffee, tea or urn, rather than the full set.

It was in the 1870's that a startling change came about, and we begin to see the influence of the Victorian period. It was a time of over-ornamentation and "fussiness" by present day standards, and it swept through home architecture, home furnishings, clothing, and many other things.

The designers of the tea sets of this period are unknown now, but they seemed to have used ornamentation for its sake alone. Totally unrelated ornamental units were used on the same piece.

An example of this is the coffee pot (Figure 5) made by the Webster Manufacturing Company of Brooklyn, New York about 1872. Here we have a stork, or crane, on the cover, a bearded viking at the top of each foot, and below the handle a ram's head with

curving horns. The chased design on the body of the pot seems to represent wheat and lilies-of-the-valley.

Another example is a pot (Figure 6) made by Simpson, Hall, Miller and Company about 1872. It has a deer's head and hoof motif for feet and an Egyptian sphinx for a cover finial.

The coffee urn in Figure 7 has a lion and shield on the cover, but the border design just under the cover inexplainably depicts palm trees and naked savages in battle with axe and spear. One man has captured a woman and is carrying her away.

Other characteristics of this period were the tall feet, "bric-a-brac" ornaments and chased designs which are almost geometric in form as in Figures 8, 9, and 10.

There must have been a wide-spread demand for this type of design, because such firms as the Meriden Britannia Company, then considered the largest silver maker in the world, supplied the mass market. They made thousands of these sets, and added new styles every few years - and, what is more, continued to do so for twenty years.

Fig. 5. A prime example of unrelated ornamentation is illustrated in this coffee pot made by the Webster Mfg. Co., about 1872. Height 9½". (Collectors of pressed glass will immediately recognize the design for the foot of this coffee pot as being the same as Hobbs, Brockunier & Company's "Centennial" pattern, also known as "Viking," and "Bearded Man" or "Bearded Head." The design patent for the "Centennial" pattern was registered by John H. Hobbs on November 21, 1876. — See A. C. Revi's "American Pressed Glass and Figure Bottles," pages 186 and 187.)

Fig. 6. Deer heads and hooves and a sphinx were used as ornaments on this teapot made by Simpson, Hall, Miller & Co., Wallingford, Conn., about 1872. Height 7 inches.

Fig. 7.   Coffee urn made by Meriden Britannia Co., about 1878. Height 18 inches.

Fig. 9.   Hand engraved teapot made by Simpson, Hall, Miller & Co., and shown in their 1878 catalog. Height 12½ inches.

Fig. 8.   This coffee pot was part of a complete tea set which was especially goldplated for a showing at the Philadelphia Centennial Exhibition in 1876. Marked "Meriden Britannia Co." Height 15 inches.

Fig. 10.   Rogers, Smith & Co. made this teapot when they were located in New Haven, Connecticut, between 1862 and 1877. Height 11".

Around 1890 another change took place. The tall feet, the unrelated ornaments, the over-embellishment, the figural finials, and meaningless chasing, all disappeared.

For a short time a repousse type of decoration, as in Figure 11, was popular. But for the most part, the tea and coffee sets were plainer with simple borders, well designed handles and spouts, and pleasingly proportioned shapes.

An attractive set was one (Figure 12) with a swirled fluted body, and simple rococo border, made by the Meriden Brittannia Company about 1896.

Even in an elaborate design like Figure 13, made by Simpson, Hall, Miller and Company of Wallingford, Connecticut, all the elements used are in harmony with each other and present a unified design pleasing to the eye.

There are some who feel that the Victorian designs in silverplate are ugly, and perhaps they are by today's standards. Without question, they are unique. And they represent a period of relaxed and gracious living which many look back to with nostalgia.

Fig. 11. Teapot made by E. G. Webster & Son. This type of ornamentation was popular for a few years around 1890. Height 7 inches.

Fig. 12. A distinctive design combining a swirled fluted body with rococo borders. Made by the Meriden Britannia Co., about 1896. Height 9¾".

Fig. 13. Simpson, Hall, Miller & Co. made this handsomely designed teapot around 1895. Height 7 inches.

Spoon holders for matched tea sets. Left to right: Meriden Silver Plate Co., ca. 1886, 6½"; Middletown Plate Co., 1867, 4¾"; Meriden Britannia Co., 1867, 6½"; Simpson, Hall, Miller & Co., 1878, 6½ inches.

Individual spoon holders not made as part of a tea set. Left to right: Middletown Plate Co., ca. 1888; Rogers, Smith & Co., ca. 1870; Barbour Silver Plate Co., early 1900s; Wilcox Silver Plate Co., 1880. Average height 6 inches.

Spoon Holders

Like the old-fashioned butter dish, spoon holders were frequently part of a tea set in Victorian silverplate. As a matter of fact, in some sets the spoon holder was furnished in place of the waste bowl. (Then inelegantly called a slop bowl.)

But, in its day, the spoon holder was considered a standard piece of equipment on the well set dining table and most silverware makers offered many additional designs from which to choose.

Most of these were about the size and shape of a goblet, but not quite as tall, and usually had two handles. There were also double spoon holders, and some in unusual shapes, as shown in the accompanying illustrations. There were some which included a bell to call the maid between courses.

Almost all of them were made entirely of metal, but a most unusual and rare one consists of a silverplated frame with a pressed glass container. This is the Tree of Life pattern in Portland glass, a product of The Portland Glass Company, Portland, Maine. They copyrighted this design in 1869.

Around 1890 there were also three piece sets called Dessert Sets, made up of sugar bowl, cream pitcher and spoon holder. Some of these had glass linings in a silverplated frame. A particularly handsome one was made by Simpson, Hall, Miller and Company of Wallingford, Connecticut in 1891. The frame was ornamented with medallions of Greecian type heads and the linings were rich ruby glass in all three pieces.

A variation of the spoon holder is one called a "Combination Spoon Holder and Sugar Bowl." This was a large sugar bowl with racks around the perimeter to hold a dozen spoons.

Spoon holders in silverplate had a comparatively long life. They date back as early as 1861, and a few were still being sold as late as 1934.

Those found in antique shops now can sometimes be distinguished from similarly shaped articles because the bottom of the inside is scarred and indented from the many spoons placed in them over the years.

They make nice little conversation pieces today, and can be used as small vases, or containers for cigarettes.

An unusual spoon holder with glass insert in the "Tree of Life" pattern; catalogued as early as 1879 by the Meriden Britannia Co.; height 5½".

No. 1441.

Chased, Gold Lined, . $5.75 (PROCREATE).
Satin, Chased, Gold Lined, 5.75 (PRODIGY).

No. 1433.

Gold Lined, . . $6.50 (LACQUER).
Old Silver, Gold Lined, 7.00 (PRODUCTION).

No. 1431.

Plain, Gold Lined, $6.75 (EXPECT).
Chased, Gold Lined, 7.50 (EXPEDIENT).

No. 1439.

Satin, Engraved, Gold Lined, $6.50 (PROBABLY).

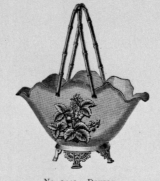

No. 1422.

Plain, Gold Lined, $5.75 (EXCEED).
Chased, . . 5.75 (EXCEL).
Chased, Gold Lined, 6.50 (EXCEPT).

No. 1435. SPOON TRAY.

Satin, Gold Lined, . $8.50 (KNAPSACK).
Hammered, Gold Lined, 10.00 (LACERATE).

No. 1442. DOUBLE.

Satin, Applied, Gold Lined, $7.50 (PRONG).
Satin, Engraved, Gold Lined, 8.50 (PROBATE).

No. 1437.

Satin, Engraved, . . $6.25 (PRIVET).
Satin, Engraved, Gold Lined, 7.00 (PRIZE).

No. 1426.

Plain, Gold Lined, $8.50 (EXACT).
Chased, . . 8.00 (EXALT).
Chased, Gold Lined, 9.50 (EXALTED).

No. 1406.

Embossed, Gold Lined, $8.50 (EXECUTE).

No. 1404.

Chased, Gold Lined, $8.50 (EXECUTOR).

(283)

Gold and Silver Plate Spoon Holders.

76

No. 1265. Gold-lined, . . . $1.15.

No. 1264, ... $1.15.

No. 1272. Chased, $5.25; gold-lined, $6.00.
No. 1272. Plain, 4.50; gold-lined, 5.25.

No. 1262. Without Spoons, $5.00.
Gold-lined, 6.50.

No. 1273. Chased, $4.25; gold-lined, $5.00.
No. 1273. Plain, 3.75; gold-lined, 4.50.

No. 1267. Chased, $6.50; gold-lined, $7.50.
No. 1267. Plain, 5.50; gold-lined, 6.50.

No. 1263. . . . $4.50.
Gold-lined, 5.50.

No. 55. Plain, $4.25; gold-lined, $5.25.
No. 55. Chased, 5.25; gold-lined, 6.25.

Nos. 1264 and 1265 are single plate and do not bear our trade-mark.

SPOON HOLDERS.

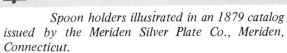

Spoon holders illustrated in an 1879 catalog issued by the Meriden Silver Plate Co., Meriden, Connecticut.

77

Double spoon holders. Left: Acorn-shaped cups with squirrel ornaments at base of handle; made by the Wilcox Silver Plate Co. about 1884; 12" high. Right: Helmet-shaped cups on an elaborate stand, also made by the Wilcox Silver Plate Co., ca. 1880; 10 inches high.

Combination sugar bowl and spoon holder. Left: Middletown Plate Co., 1879; 8½" high. Right: Meriden Britannia Co., ca. 1896; 8½" high.

SPITTOONS.

Parlor.

Ring and Feet.   Ring.

No. 1, Parlor, extra fine rolled metal,   .   .   per dozen, $14.25

Ring and Feet,   Cast   "   .   .   "   9.50

Ring,   "   "   .   .   "   8.81

No. 374.   Cuspidor, $16.00. (MENACING
Roman Gold-Inlaid and gold-lined,   26.00. (MENAGE

Britannia metal Spittoons (both rolled and cast) made by the Meriden Britannia Co. in 1855. These were unplated, but only a few years later, the company was making them in silverplate.

Reed and Barton of Taunton, Mass. were offering these handsome styles in 1885. Not only were they silverplated, but parts of the ornamentation were in what was called "Roman Gold-Inlaid"; they were also gold-lined.

No. 374.   Spittoon, $15.00. (MERCE
Roman Gold-Inlaid and gold-lined,   24.00. (MERCEN

Oddities

A hundred years from now, when historians look back to the Twentieth Century, many things about our present way of life will doubtless seem odd and strange.

And so it is with us, when we look back a hundred or so years in the field of silverware. Some of the things which were then thought to be necessary, or at least desirable, have no place in our lives today.

Vast changes have come about in the processing, storage, packaging, and merchandising of foods. And in transportation, communications and health. These changes have brought about corresponding changes in our dining habits and mode of living.

The Spitoon or Cuspidor

Years before and years after 1842, when Charles Dickens visited America, the practice of chewing tobacco and the consequent spitting was an American characteristic which appalled foreign visitors to our shores. Charles Dickens has this to say in his *"American Notes,"* published in 1842:

> "Several gentlemen called upon me who, in the course of the conversation, frequently missed the spitoon at five paces, and one, (but he was certainly short sighted) mistook the closed sash for the open window at three."

Another English writer, Harriet Martineau (1802–1876) traveled in America in 1834, and wrote about it in a fair and conservative way. In her book, *"Society in America"* she wrote:

> "Of tobacco and its consequences I will say nothing but that the practice is at too bad a pass to leave hope that anything that could be said in books would work a cure. If the floors of boarding houses, and the decks of steamboats, and the carpets of the Capitol do not sicken the Americans into reform; if the warnings of physicians are of no avail, what remains to be said? I dismiss the nauseous subject."

This unpleasant habit, however, led to the need for spitoons or cuspidors, and while many of these were made in tin and china, or ceramics of some sort, they were also made in silverplate. The Meriden Britannia Company, a predecessor of International Silver Company, was organized in 1852, and in their first price list, issued in 1853, they listed seven different numbers in britannia metal. In 1861, they were offering "parlor spitoons," silverplated on white metal at three dollars and thirty-seven and one-half cents each.

Other makers, such as Meriden Silver Plate Company, E. G. Webster and Bro., and Reed and Barton, also made them even as late as 1886.

Porcupine
Tooth Pick Holder.

Each, $1 50.
Gilt. Each, $2 00.

Tooth Pick Holder

Before tooth picks were· used primarily for holding club sandwiches together, or spearing hors d'oeuvres at a cocktail party, picking one's teeth was apparently a more common practice than it is today.

Many homes had silver tooth pick holders on the dining table, and these were frequently attractive little containers, ornamented with animals, birds, children, etc.

The earliest tooth picks were quills, so perhaps it is logical that an early holder for them was made in the form of a porcupine. This unique piece was first offered by the Meriden Britannia Company in 1867. However, it was evidently sold to other makes as well who marketed it with their own trademark. (See accompanying illustration of one sold by Wilcox Silver Plate Company. This was cataloged by them in 1868.)

No. 12.

Old Silver, . . $3.75 (PRECLUDE).

The "mouse" match safe made by Meriden Britannia Co. in 1873. Width 5 inches.

Match Safes

Another small object of interest is the match safe. Today, when we have electric stoves and automatic pilots on gas stoves, and lighters for our cigarettes, the need for matches is not as great. In the days of the old fashioned kitchen match, match safes were made in silverplate, and some of them used the figure of a mouse as a knob on the cover. The significance of this, presumably, was that a mouse nibbling the old fashioned match heads could cause fire, and the only safe place to keep them was in a match safe.

An Unusual Tea Pot

The silver tea pot is one thing which has survived the years, and is perhaps as popular today as it was years ago - but there was one style that did not survive. This, perhaps was more of a novelty than anything else, and it was called the "self pouring tea pot" or "pump pot."

Paine, Diehl and Company of Philadelphia, through some arrangement, obtained the right to sell a unique type of tea pot made under what was known as Royle's Patent. They were listed as hardware dealers and commission merchants in the city directories from 1883 to 1895.

Not being manufacturers themselves, they came to the Meriden Britannia Company and commissioned them to make five different designs for them in silverplate. This they did by adapting standard catalog designs to fit the patented construction. One of these is shown in the accompanying illustration. Tea was pumped into the cup by moving the cover up and down. (A "pumping" cylinder was attached to the cover).

Self-pouring teapot, silverplate, made by the Meriden Britannia Co., in 1886, for Paine, Diehl & Co., Philadelphia.

The Sardine Box

If, in the course of your visits to antique shops, you run across a little box with a fish finial on the cover, it is probably a sardine box. Why it was thought desirable to have a special box from which to serve sardines, we do not know - but the fact is they were made by such predecessors of International Silver as Meriden Silver Plate Company, Middletown Plate Company, Wilcox Silver Plate Company, Simpson, Hall, Miller and Company, and Meriden Britannia Company from as early as 1861 to about 1890.

Sardine Boxes from the 1886 catalog of the Meriden Britannia Co. Average width about 6 inches. Overhead handle styles are about 9 inches tall.

(One-Third Size.)

No. 05.
Nickel Silver, Silver Soldered, $13.50 (PHANTOM).

No. 1876, . . $10.00 (PHENIX).

No. 1867.

Satin, . .	$5.00	(PHIAL).
Engraved, . .	6.00	(PHILTER).
Hammered, . .	6.00	(PHRASE).
Hammered, and Applied,	6.50	(PHYSIC).

No. 1878, . . $10.00 (PERTAIN).

No. 1880, . . $10.50 (PERTINENT).

No. 1881, . . $11.50 (PERUKE).

No. 1874, Satin, Engraved, $10.50 (PICA).

No. 1877, . . $12.00 (PICTURE).

No. 1875, . . $10.50 (PICKET).

SARDINE TONGS, $1.50 each (see Flat Ware) (PICNIC).

*Sardine Boxes as shown by Simpson, Hall,
Miller & Co. (Wallingford, Conn.) in 1878. Average
width about 6 inches. Overhead handle styles are
about 9 inches tall.*

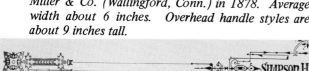

Fine Cut Glass.
No. 35. Sardine Box.
$7.50.

Fine Cut Glass.
No. 40. Sardine Box.
$6.50.

Fine Cut Glass.
No. 30. Sardine Box.
$6.00.

No. 25. Sardine Box. Ivy Chased.
Plain, ... $4.25.
Chased, ... 5.00.

No. 10. Mustard Pot.
$3.50.

No. 70. Cheese Dish.
Fine Cut Glass Cover.
$8.00.

No. 10. Gravy Boat.
$7.00.

Sardine Boxes, Mustard Pot, Gravy Boat, Cheese Dish, Etc.

Celery Stands

Celery must have been a popular food in Victorian days, and silver makers, not to miss an opportunity, designed special stands to hold the stalks for serving on the dining table.

Here again, this is one of the early pieces made in silverplate, going back to the 1860's. The early styles were very attractive, shaped like a goblet with two handles usually, and containing an insert of cut, pressed, or colored glass in a great variety of designs. They ranged from six inches to ten inches tall.

In the 1870's, as was true of much of the silverplate, the designs became more elaborate and flamboyant. The glass inserts were more attractive and imaginative, however, and the general overall effect is charming.

By 1893, the popularity of this type seems to have waned and silver makers were then offering long flat dishes called celery trays.

CELERY STANDS.

PLATED ON WHITE METAL.

No. 6.

Each, . . $10 00

No. 0100.

PLATED ON NICKEL SILVER.

Each, . . $20 00

No. 7.

Each, . . . $10 50

No. 5, X.

Each, . . $12 75

No. 8.

Each, . . $7 50

No. 5.

Each, . . . $12 00

No. 60.
Ruby, Decorated, $10.50 (REPLENISH).

No. 63.
Venetian Thread Glass, $8.50 (PAYABLE).
Assorted Colors.

No. 59.
Decorated, . $9.50 (REFINE).
Assorted Colors.

No. 55, . $8.50 (DAMSON).

No. 53. . $11.00 (DANCE).
Crystal Cut.

No. 61.
Decorated, . $12.50 (REPEL).
Assorted Colors.

No. 57.
Crystal, Cut, . $10.50 (REPEATER).

No. 62.
Crystal, Engraved, . $11.00 (REPEAT).

No. 58.
Decorated, . $10.50 (REPLACE).
Assorted Colors.

Opposite: A few of the many styles of Celery Stands cataloged by the Meriden Britannia Co. in 1886. They ranged in height from 6 to 10 inches.

Rogers, Smith & Co. of New Haven were making these Celery Stands in 1867.

Pepper Boxes

Compared to salt, which goes back to ancient times, pepper as a table seasoning is a recent arrival.

The first written reference to salt is in the Bible in the Book of Job, which was written about three hundred years before the birth of Christ.

Pepper and other spices in whole form were imported to America from earliest Colonial days, but ground pepper did not come into use until 1837, when Slade Brothers set up a mill in Chelsea, Massachusetts and started to grind and sell a variety of spices.

In the early days, salt was placed on the table in small containers called "open salts" or "salt cellars." In silver, these usually had colored glass linings and a tiny individual salt spoon for serving.

When ground pepper came into use, the serving piece was at first called a pepper box. This term was chiefly British in origin, and simply signified a vessel with a perforated top for shaking pepper on to food. Maybe the first ones were actually boxes, but even after they took on the traditional shaker form they were, for a while, still called pepper boxes.

As they did in so many other things, the makers of silverplate in the last half of the Nineteenth Century, designed some of these pepper containers in amusing shapes. There were boys and girls, dogs and cats, bottles and jugs, and parrots, and hats.

The novelty shapes seem to have faded out by 1891, and the matching pairs of salt and pepper shakers in traditional shapes took their place.

Some people collect the old silver-plated pepper boxes as a hobby. There is no way of knowing how popular they were, or how many were made, but they do seem to be scarce in the antique shops today.

The Meriden Silver Plate Co. showed these pepper "boxes" in their catalog for 1884. Sizes 1½ to 3 inches tall.

No. 770.
Silver, $1.00. (HOPPER)
Gilt, 1.25. (HOPING)
Old Silver, 1.25. (HORIZON)
Old Sil. & Gilt, 1.50. (HORN)

No. 784.
Silver, $2.00. (STRIDE)
Gilt, 2.50. (STRIFE)
XX Gilt, 3.00. (STRING)

No. 779.
Silver, $1.75. (HOUND)
Old Silver, 2.00. (HOUR)
Old Sil. & Sil., 2.25. (HOUSE)
Old Sil. & Gilt, 2.50. (HOVEL)

No. 765.
Silver, $2.25. (HOOD)
Oxidized, 2.50. (HOOK)
Gilt, 2.75. (HOOF)

No. 781.
Silver, $2.00. (HUCKSTER)
Gilt, 2.25. (HUDDLE)

No. 778.
Silver, $1.50. (HOSTILE)
Gilt, 1.75. (HOSTLER)
Old Silver, 1.75. (HOTEL)
Old Sil. & Gilt, 2.00. (HOTSPUR)

No. 780.
Silver, $1.00. (HOWITZER)
Gilt, 1.25. (HOWL)

No. 146.
Salt, $1.25. (CAREFUL)

No. 773.
Silver, $1.50. (HORRID)
Gilt Top, 1.75. (HORRIFY)

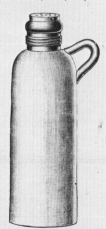

No. 771.
Gilt Top, $2.25. (HORNET)
Hammered, 2.50. (SPARK)
Hammered, Applied and Gilt, 3.00. (SPARROW)

No. 774.
Silver, $1.50. (HORSE)
Gilt, 1.75. (HOSE)

No. 772.
Gilt Top, $2.50. (HORRIBLE)
XX Gilt, 3.25. (TOKEN)

No. 762.
Longwy, $1.00. (HONEST)

No. 785.
Silver, $2.50. (STROKE)
Gilt, 3.00. (STROLL)
XX Gilt, 3.50. (STRONG)

No. 70.

Silver, . . . $1.00 (CURB).
X Gilt, . . . 1.25 (CURDLE).

No. 67.

Silver, . . . $1.00 (COUNTERPLOT).
Silver, Gilt Cap, 1.25 (COUNTERSIGN).

No. 68.

Silver, . . . $1.00 (COUNTRYSEAT).
Oxidized and Gilt, 1.25 (COUNTERSCARP).
Gilt, . . . 1.50 (COUNTERVAIL).

No. 71.

Silver, . . . $2.00 (CURRY).
X Gilt, . . . 2.25 (CURTAIL).

No. 69.

Silver, . . . $2.00 (CURRICLE).
X Gilt, . . . 2.50 (CURRIER).

No. 04. PEPPER OR SALT.
Nickel Silver.

Silver Top, . . . $1.25 (COUNTLESS).
Gilt Top, . . . 1.50 (COURAGEOUS).

No. 72.

Old Silver, . $2.25 (CURE).
X Gilt, . . . 2.75 (CURFEW).
X Gilt, Oxidized, 3.00 (CURIOUS).

No. 65.

Silver, . $2.00 (COUNTERPOISE).
Gilt, . . 2.50 (COUNTERPART).

No. 66.

Silver, . $2.00 (COUNSEL).
Gilt, . . 2.50 (COUNTENANCE).

No. 73.

Old Silver, . . $2.25 (CURL).
X Gilt, . . . 2.75 (CURLEW).
X Gilt, Oxidized, 3.00 (CURRANT).

Pepper "boxes" offered by the Meriden Britannia Co. in 1886. The little girl and boy are patterned after Kate Greenaway's illustrations, and are the same figures used on napkin rings. Heights range from 2 to 4 inches.

Mustache Cups

Old photographs and portraits of the Nineteenth Century clearly show how a great portion of the male population then sported beards or flowing mustaches. Apparently it was the ambition of most young men, at that time, to graduate as soon as possible from the class of "beardless youths."

This led to the introduction of mustache cups. This was a coffee or tea cup with a small bar, or lip, inside which shielded the mustache from the liquid. They were most common, of course, in china or pottery, but they were made in silverplate too.

It would seem an impractical idea to serve a hot beverage in a metal cup, but they must have been fairly popular because they were offered by several of the silver makers from about 1886 to 1899.

Another curious piece which this hirsute fashion inspired was a mustache spoon. This was patented August 8, 1890, and was offered in the *LINDEN* and *WINDSOR* patterns in 1847 Rogers Bros. Silverplate. Called the "etiquette" spoon and described as "the most perfect mustache spoon ever made."

It was made in teaspoon and dessert spoon sizes, and both right hand and left hand. Apparently it was never very popular, because it is not mentioned in later catalogs.

No. 7. MOUSTACHE.

Plain, ... $6.50 (FOLIAGE).
Plain, Gold Lined Cup, 7.25 (FOLIO).
Chased, . . . 9.00 (FOLK).
Chased, Gold Lined Cup, 9.75 (FOLLOW).

No. 8. MOUSTACHE.
Satin, Gold Lined Cup, . . $6.50 (PIGMENT).
Brocade Chased, Gold Lined Cup, 8.00 (PIGEON).

Mustache Cups made by Meriden Britannia Co. in 1886. Saucers are about 6 inches in diameter.

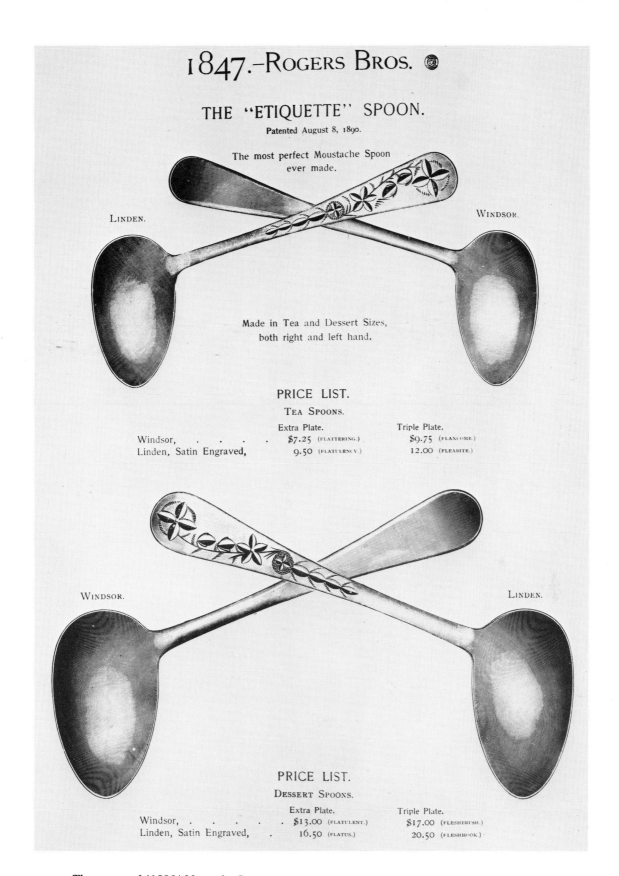

1847.-ROGERS BROS.

THE "ETIQUETTE" SPOON.

Patented August 8, 1890.

The most perfect Moustache Spoon
ever made.

LINDEN.

WINDSOR.

Made in Tea and Dessert Sizes,
both right and left hand.

PRICE LIST.
TEA SPOONS.

	Extra Plate.	Triple Plate.
Windsor, ...	$7.25 (FLATTERING.)	$9.75 (FLAXCOMB.)
Linden, Satin Engraved,	9.50 (FLATULENCY.)	12.00 (FLEABITE.)

WINDSOR.

LINDEN.

PRICE LIST.
DESSERT SPOONS.

	Extra Plate.	Triple Plate.
Windsor, ...	$13.00 (FLATULENT.)	$17.00 (FLESHBRUSH.)
Linden, Satin Engraved, .	16.50 (FLATUS.)	20.50 (FLESHHOOK.)

The patented (1890) Mustache Spoon in two patterns, two sizes, and two styles (left and right) shown in the 1893 catalog of 1847 Rogers Bros. Silverplate.

Orange Peelers

Oranges must have been a very popular fruit in the old days and our ancestors paid particular attention to the manner in which they were served. Often times they were cut in half as we now serve grapefruit and placed in small silver plated "orange cups" shaped like sherbets. Some of these had patented devices to hold the orange in place.

There were orange spoons with especially shaped bowls for eating the sections and these spoons were sometimes made in special patterns. There were orange knives with "saw-backs" and several styles on which the blade had a forked end for removing seeds.

One of the most unusual pieces was the orange-peeler of which there were a number of patented designs. Two of these are shown in the accompanying illustrations. One was made in both table and pocket sizes.

Today one would find it almost impossible to identify the use of these "tools" without having access to old silverware catalogs.

First Operation.

Second Operation.

This orange peeler was patented in 1879 and made by Holmes, Booth and Haydens. They were established in 1853 in Waterbury, Connecticut. In 1886 they were bought by Rogers and Hamilton, which, in turn, became part of International Silver Co. in 1898.

HOLMES, BOOTH & HAYDENS, 21

ORANGE PEELER.

PATENTED AUGUST, 1879.

In offering the above ingenious device to the Trade, it being the only one ever invented, warrants the manufacturer in believing it will fill a want the Orange-loving public have long felt. Who has not experienced the necessity for something of the kind, when compelled to peel this luscious fruit (for want of a better means) with thumb and fingers?

IT CERTAINLY IS AN ARTICLE that, soon as known, will be recognized as a necessity in every first-class Hotel, Restaurant and Private Family, consequently must have a large and ready sale, especially in all orange-growing countries.

It is made of Nickel Silver, extra heavily plated, and warranted in every respect. Price, $12.00 per dozen.

Discount to the Trade.

A PRACTICAL NOVELTY.

The ORANGE PEELER hereon illustrated is conceded by all who have used it to be perfect in its operation, neatly removing the peel without soiling the fingers.

Made in table and pocket sizes, assorted patterns and finishes. Table size put up six in plush lined paper box; pocket size each in leather sheath in paper box.

PRICE FOR EACH SIZE $6.00 PER DOZEN.

SPECIAL DISCOUNT TO THE TRADE.

DIRECTIONS FOR USING.

Hold the Peeler in the right hand, Orange in left, with thumb of right hand on orange as shown in cut; with flat face of hook placed square on orange, draw with pressure enough to insert hook in and under peel, revolve orange in left hand, drawing peeler in opposite direction until peel is cut into as many sections as desired, when it may be easily removed by inserting back of peeler under loose point of section. The blade on back of peeler is useful for removing the soft white under skin.

ROGERS & BROTHER,

16 CORTLANDT STREET,

NEW YORK.

One of several patented Orange Peelers. This one was patented in 1893. The style on the left was approximately 5 inches long, and was called the table size. The pocket style, on the right, was about 3¾ inches long.

Five piece place setting in 1847 Rogers Bros. Vintage pattern.

Vintage Flatware

All over America today there are hundreds of people who pursue the fascinating hobby of collecting old patterns in silverplate.

So many thousands of patterns have been made since the year 1847, when silverplate first came on the market, that the field is limitless. And the best part about it is that silverplate of this type is relatively inexpensive, and can easily be found in antique shops, Salvation Army and Goodwill stores.

Some people collect indiscriminately - any pattern that pleases their fancy. Some collect just teaspoons in as many patterns as possible. Some confine their activity to just one trademark, such as 1847 Rogers Bros., and some specialize in patterns with "grape" ornamentation.

In this latter class, the pattern which is the most popular by far is the one named *VINTAGE*. There are other patterns with a grape motif, but only one *VINTAGE*.

This pattern was designed by Samuel Stohr, a staff designer for International Silver Company, and patented August 2, 1904, Number 37059. It was made by the Meriden Britannia Company and first introduced in 1904 under the trademark 1847 Rogers Bros. It was discontinued about 1918.

VINTAGE was a great success from the start, and in 1905, the year following its introduction, some sixty-five different items were being made. As the popularity of the pattern increased, new items were added, so that by 1915 or 1916, they reached the almost unbelievable total of one hundred and one different "tools" for eating and serving food.

Unusual Pieces

All the standard knives, forks and spoons were made, of course, but in addition, there were a great many other pieces. How many of these unusual pieces were actually sold is a question. In any event, they were made and offered in catalogs of the period. A few of these unusual pieces were:

Chocolate Muddler
Egg Spoon
Cracker Spoon
Ice Spoon
Pea Spoon
Fish Knives and Forks (both flat handle and hollow handle, both individual and serving)
Cake and Bread Knives
Seven kinds of Ladles
Bottle Opener
Lobster Pick
Asparagus Tongs
Sugar Sifter
Roast Holder
Poultry Shears
Knife Sharpener
Cheese Scoop

Types of Knives

When *VINTAGE* first came out, only the hollow handle knives were offered in two sizes - medium and dessert.

These hollow handles were formed of two shells of nickle silver, joined together with silver solder. Blades of crucible steel were inserted. Stainless steel blades had not yet been invented. These were the best knives, comfortable to hold, and bearing good sharp pattern detail.

Later, a third size, called a breakfast knife, was introduced. The medium (dinner) size was nine and one-half inches; the breakfast, nine inches; and the dessert, eight and one-half inches long. In 1915, they were priced at sixteen dollars, fifteen dollars and fifty cents, and fifteen dollars per dozen respectively.

That same year, a cheaper knife was offered in medium and dessert sizes. This was called a "solid handle" knife, and both blade and handle were forged in one piece from a rod of steel. Because of the difficulty in stamping hard steel, the pattern delineation is not as sharp as in the better quality. Solid handle medium knives sold for seven dollars and fifty cents a dozen, and the dessert size, seven dollars and thirty cents.

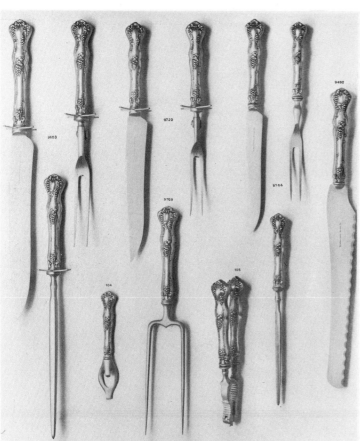

Left to Right: All hollow handle Meat Carving Knife and Fork, Game Carving Knife and Fork, Bread Knife. Below: Meat Carving Steel (for Sharpening Knife), Bottle Opener, Roast Holder, Nut Crack, Breakfast Carving Steel.

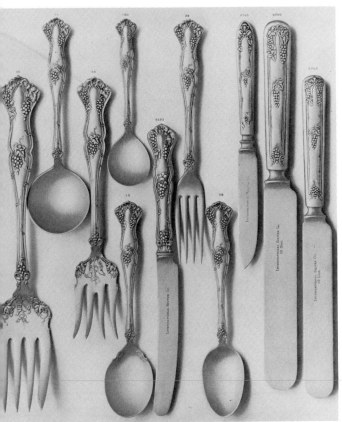

Left to Right: Cold Meat Fork, Bouillon Spoon, Beef Fork, Chocolate Spoon, Ice Cream Spoon (below), Child's Knife (hollow handle), Child's Fork, Child's Spoon, Fruit Knife (solid handle), Medium Knife (solid handle), Dessert Knife (solid handle).

Left to Right: Medium Knife (hollow handle), Dessert Fork, Coffee Spoon, Egg Spoon (below), Tea Spoon, Table Spoon, Orange Spoon, Dessert Spoon, Medium Fork, Fruit Knife (hollow handle), Dessert Knife (hollow handle).

Left to Right: Butter Spreader, Berry Spoon, Sugar Shell, Cream Ladle, Gravy Ladle, Butter Knife (twist), Soup Spoon, Ice Spoon, Cheese Scoop (hollow handle).

Left to Right: Iced Tea Spoon, Asparagus Tongs (hollow handle), Pickle Fork (long), Fish Knife, Salad Fork (Ind.), Oyster Fork, Olive Spoon.

Quality Marks

In 1904, it was the practice to make teaspoons, dessert spoons, table spoons, dessert forks and medium forks in three different qualities. These were called Extra Plate, Sectional or XII Plate, and Triple Plate. (Other pieces were made only in Extra and Triple Plate.)

Extra Plate was "plated twenty percent heavier than ordinary standard," and was trademarked "1847 Rogers Bros. AI."

Sectional or XII Plate was plated "three times the usual thickness on parts most exposed to wear" (tip of bowl, and backs of bowls and handles.) This quality was stamped "1847 Rogers Bros. XII."

Triple Plate was plated "three times the usual thickness over the whole spoon or fork," and marked "1847 Rogers Bros. 6" (for teaspoons) and the numerals 9 and 12 for the correspondingly larger pieces.

In 1909, without increasing prices, all the qualities were up-graded. The former Extra Plate was increased to Triple Plate and marked XS Triple. The Sectional Plate was given additional plating and marked XII-XS Triple. The former Triple Plate was increased to "five times the usual thickness" and changed to XS Quintuple.

In addition, there appears a small round mark, usually too small to distinguish. This is actually the trademark (a pair of scales in a circle) of the Meriden Britannia Company, which had been making 1847 Rogers Bros. Silverplate since 1862.

In 1917, all these qualifying marks were discontinued and only one quality, heavier than ever before, was made from that time on.

A dozen *VINTAGE* teaspoons in XS Triple quality cost four dollars and seventy-five cents; in Sectional five dollars and fifty cents; and in XS Quintuple, six dollars and fifty cents.

Another "grape" pattern popular with collectors, and which was current about the same time as *VINTAGE*, is one called *MOS-ELLE*. This was made in "World Brand" and was a product of the American Silver Company of Bristol, Connecticut.

The antecedents of this firm were the Holmes and Tuttle Manufacturing Company, founded in 1851. They were taken over by the Bristol Brass and Clock Company in 1857, and operated as their silverware department until 1901. In that year, the spoon business was separated from the brass and clock business, and organized under the name of the American Silver Company. They were bought by International Silver Company in 1935.

MOSELLE is a very attractive pattern, and when it was active, about sixty different pieces were made.

Still another "grape" pattern is *LA VIGNE*, bearing the trademark 1881 (wreath) Rogers (wreath.) This mark came into use about 1910, and had no connection with the original Rogers brothers. The trademark is the property of Oneida, Limited, Oneida, New York.

Of less importance is the pattern called *ISABELLA*, which was made in a very inexpensive brand in the early 1900's (ca. 1915) under the trademark R. C. Co. It was a product of the Rogers Cutlery Company, founded in Hartford, Connecticut in 1871, and later a division of International Silver Company. A limited amount of this pattern was also sold with the trademark Wm. Rogers and Son.

It is phenomenal, in a way, that any pattern in silverplate should enjoy such popularity more than half a century after it had been discontinued. But *VINTAGE* does, (albeit in a restricted field) and antique shops and dealers who specialize in supplying discontinued patterns find a ready market for pieces which turn up from time to time.

"La Vigne" pattern made by Oneida, Ltd. of Oneida, N. Y., under their Rogers trademark.
"Moselle" pattern made by American Silver Co., Bristol, Conn.

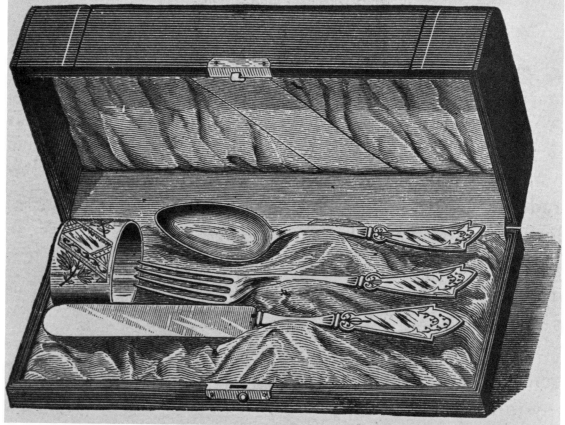

Three piece Child's Set in "Princess" pattern with napkin ring illustrated in the Meriden Britannia Co. catalog for 1879.

Three piece Child's Set on card shown in Meriden Britannia Co. catalog for 1887. The pattern is "Fairie."

Three piece Child's Set on colorful, lithographed card offered by Meriden Britannia Co. in 1887. The pattern is "Assyrian."

Children's Silverware

A study of old catalogs of silverplate issued seventy-five to one hundred years ago cannot fail to impress the reader with the almost unbelievable array of articles made and offered for sale.

This was particularly true during the 1870's and 1880's. In every situation pertaining to the serving and consumption of food and beverages, personal grooming and adornment and furnishings and ornaments for the home there was silverware to make living more gracious and pleasant. Indeed, from child's cups and child's sets to crematory urns and casket hardware the silverware makers were prepared to serve everyone in elegant style, from the cradle to the grave.

Although the research for this article is limited to the records of the International Silver Company and its predecessors, the Meriden Britannia Company was the largest silverware company in the world and 1847 Rogers Bros. silverplate the leading brand.

It is not unreasonable to assume that other silverware makers of the period proceeded along similar lines insofar as they were able.

Flatware for Children

When the Rogers Brothers first advertised their silverplate in 1847 there was nothing at all made especially for children and even by 1855 the Meriden Britannia Company (founded in 1852) confined their flatware offering to some twenty-one different items in five patterns - all for adult use.

But by 1860, the Rogers Bros. Mfg. Co. of Hartford, Connecticut started to cater to the juvenile market and list a "Beef or Child's Fork" in four patterns - *BEADED, OLIVE, DOUBLE THREADED* and *OVAL THREADED.* No special child's spoon is listed and apparently the regular teaspoon was used. They also listed 3-piece sets of spoon, fork and knife in the *OVAL* and *OLIVE* patterns.

In the years 1875 through 1879 (by this time 1847 Rogers Bros. silverplate was being made in Meriden, Connecticut by the Meriden Britannia Company) still no special child's spoon was being made but Beef or Child's Forks were offered in ten different patterns as well as a Child's Knife. These were listed as "Flat Handle, used also as small Tea or Fruit Knives."

In that latter year boxed sets were shown including 3-piece sets consisting of spoon, fork and a choice of flat handle knife, pearl handle knife or silverplated steel knife.

There were also "School Sets" which included, in addition, a napkin ring and a cup, and even a "College Set" which was made up of a teaspoon, dessert spoon, dessert size knife and fork and a napkin ring all packed in a handsome morocco case.

Through the 1880's child's sets were made in an increasing number of patterns and even in special patterns such as "Fairie" in which no other pieces were made. The makers became "display-minded" too and mounted sets on colorful cards depicting childhood scenes and also packed sets in special boxes with colored pictures on the cover.

During all this time there seems to have been nothing at all especially for babies. The curved or bent handle baby spoon, as well as the short straight handle spoon and fork (called the Educator Set) was introduced in the *VINTAGE* pattern in 1904. Even three years later the bent handle spoon was only being offered in three of the eleven patterns current at that time. But it became more popular as the years went by and by 1926 was a standard catalog item in all 1847 Rogers Bros. patterns.

Around 1941 with the growing popularity of the prepared baby food, a new spoon was introduced. This had a small, oval bowl to fit tiny mouths and a long handle to facilitate feeding from the jars. It was instantly popular and called an Infant Feeding Spoon.

Left to Right: Sterling silver food pusher "Revere" pattern. Baby spoon with Mickey Mouse design. Baby Fork "Silver Fashion" pattern. Infant Feeding Spoon "Silver Fashion" pattern. Bent handle Baby Spoon "Old Colony" Pattern. (Infant Feeding Spoon is 5" in length).

Child's Set in "Assyrian" pattern made in 1847 Rogers Bros. silverplate introduced in 1887.

Food Pushers

The food pusher, shaped like a little rake without teeth, was introduced in 1893 in two patterns -- *DUNDEE* and *PORTLAND*. Almost always shown in relation to children's silverware, a popular combination consisted of the bent handle spoon and food pusher retailing at two dollars in 1905.

It was usually made in all current patterns until about 1929 when it appears to have been discontinued.

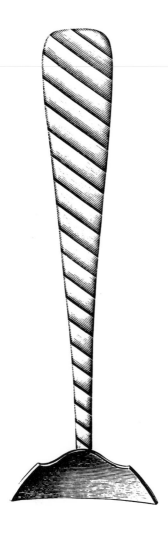

Food Pushers in "Dundee" (left) and "Portland" (right) patterns as shown in 1893. Length 3½".

Child's Cups

Child's cups on the other hand were among the earliest pieces made in silverplate and grew to be one of the most popular.

The first illustrated catalog put out by the Meriden Britannia Company in 1855, three years after they were organized, shows only one style but it was offered five different ways - in plain britannia metal (unplated), silverplated, goldplated inside, engraved and engraved and goldplated inside.

The Rogers Mfg. Co. of Hartford, Connecticut showed two attractive designs in 1857. Each following year saw new designs being offered and by 1877 the Meriden Britannia Company illustrated twenty-two different cups.

This grew to forty-six in 1882 and to fifty-nine different styles in 1886. Most of them followed the decorative styles used on other pieces of the period but some were ornamented with figures of birds, animals, children and even snakes.

In addition to cups there were child's trays and pap bowls (for cereal and bread and milk) and baby plates which came on the scene about 1880.

Children's Cups as shown in the 1860 Rogers Bros. Mfg. Co. catalog.

Child's cups. Top row, left to right: Meriden Britannia Co.; 1882. Rogers & Bro.; 1870. Rogers & Bro. (snake handle); 1880. Hartford Silver Plate Co.; 1880. Bottom row, left to right; Superior Silver Co.; 1890. Meriden Britannia Co.; 1867. Wm. Rogers Mfg. Co.; 1896. Rogers & Bro.; 1882. Dates are approximate. Largest cup is 4" tall. smallest cup is 2" tall.

NO. 126. BREAD AND MILK BOWL, WITH SPOON.
"Hammered" and "Antique."

Plain, ... $8.50 (Gainless)
"Hammered" and Gold Lined, ... 9.50 (Gainsay)
"   " Fancy Gilt, ... 10.50 (Gaiter)
Height, 3 inches.

NO. 127. CHILD'S BOWL, SAUCER AND SPOON.
In Fine Case. Basket Finish, Old Silver and Gold Lined.
$10.00 (Morality)
Price of Case, $2.50 net, extra.
Height of bowl, 3 inches. Diameter of saucer, 5¼ inches.

NO. 30. CHILD'S BOWL, SAUCER AND SPOON.
In Fine Leather Case, Etched, Old Silver and Gold Finish.
With Gold Lined Bowl, $12.00 (Lovable)
Price of Case, $2.50 net, extra.
Height of bowl, 3 inches.
Diameter of saucer, 6 inches.

NO. 128. CHILD'S BOWL, SAUCER AND SPOON.
In Fine Case.
Engraved, Silver Finish, ... $7.50 (Moran)
"   " "   and Gold Lined, . 9.50 (Moravian)
"   Old Silver and Gilt, ... 10.50 (Morbid)
Price of Case, $2.50 net, extra.
Height of bowl, 3¼ inches. Diameter of saucer, 5¼ inches.

Simpson, Hall, Miller & Co. illustrated these children's bowls in their 1891 catalog.

Child's Trays illustrated in Meriden Britannia Co. catalog for 1886 ranged in size from 16½" to 18" in length.

Royal Baby Plate

An unusual metal baby plate was invented by John J. Benson of Detroit, Michigan and patented by him February 7, 1905 under design patent Number D701,789. Mr. Benson assigned the patent to Royal Baby Plate Company of New York City.

The chief construction feature of this plate was the upper edge or rim which curved inward so that the food fell into the plate instead of on the floor or table. It was also advertised as the "plate that can't tip over."

Meriden Britannia Company, apparently under some licensing agreement, made this in silverplate under their own trademark as well as that of Rogers, Smith and Company and 1847 Rogers Bros. Under the Forbes Silver Company mark it was illustrated in catalogs continuously from 1908 through 1930. It was also made in sterling silver.

It was made in a plain style and also with various decorations around the rim.

These included alphabet blocks, animals, nursery rhyme figures, etc. Then again in 1933, for a few years, it was made with a Mickey Mouse decoration.

Beginning around 1930, with the coming of more sophisticated ideas in packaging and more aggressive methods of merchandising, literally hundreds of different juvenile sets were introduced in the major lines of both silverplate and sterling silver.

These took the basic child's sets, baby spoons, educator sets and cups and combined them with all manner of novelties and toys of cloth, wood, papier-mache, cardboard, plastic and china all attractively gift boxed in the then new, transparent plastic. This was also the period of special juvenile silverware reproducing cartoon characters such as Mickey Mouse, Skippy, Pop Eye, Snow White, and others too numerous to mention.

The "Royal Baby Plate" made under the Forbes Silver Co. trademark from 1908 through 1930; diameter 8½ inches.

My Own Set

A plate now beginning to turn up among collectors is a china one originally made by the Salem China Company of Salem, Ohio. It has a little extension on each side - the one on the left reading - "I go here says the fork." - and on the right - "I go here says the spoon." (There was also a Spanish language edition for sale in the export market.)

This plate was the idea of J. Leo Dowd, then Sales Manager for Holmes and Edwards Silverplate, patented in 1932 under his name (Number 88343) and assigned to International Silver Company. It was made exclusively for the Holmes and Edwards Division and marketed with a two-piece Educator Set under the name of "My Own Set."

After the Salem China Company was sold the plate was made, under the same patent, by the Homer Laughlin China Company of Newell, West Virginia.

Beginning in 1954 the "My Own Set" was offered with the plate decorated with colorful pictures of Betsy McCall and Jimmie Weeks - characters popularized and copyrighted by McCalls magazine. Although this style was available for several years it never attained the popularity of the original set which continued in the line for thirty-seven years.

During its life several hundred thousand plates were sold, all with two-piece Educator Sets, a rather remarkable record for a juvenile item.

Silverware for children, while not now merchandised to the extent it was thirty-five to forty years ago is still made in sterling, silverplate and even stainless steel and doubtless, like children, will always be with us.

The "My Own Set" put out by Holmes & Edwards Silver Co. Pattern is "Danish Princess"; introduced in 1938.

A splendid example of the elaborate card
receivers of the 1880's. This one was made by the
Meriden Silver Plate Co. in 1884.

The cornucopia-shaped vase of blue opaline
glass is decorated with designs in white enamel and
gold. A winged elf reins in a small bird.

Card Receivers

One of the most intriguing pieces of Victorian silverplate is called a "Card Receiver." It was an extremely popular piece in its day, made by all the silverware makers. Perhaps no other single item was made in such great variety in size and form and elaborateness of decoration.

In the 1860's a generally practiced social custom was "visiting" or "paying calls" on friends and acquaintances. And whether or not the "visitee" was at home, the visitor left her card in a small receptacle on the hall table, provided for the purpose.

So widespread was the custom that even in far away and sparsely settled Alaska, and as late as 1911, women observed this example of correct etiquette.

Margaret A. Murie in her book *Two in the Far North* published by Alfred A. Knopf, Inc., describes life in Fairbanks, Alaska in 1911. (She was nine years old.):

"The respectable society of Fairbanks was very proper. Every house, no matter how small, had a 'card tray' on a little stand by the door, and the ladies all left cards, another fascinating little facet of life for a small girl. After the callers had left, I would study the cards - 'Mrs. Louis Kossuth Pratt', 'Mrs. John Knox Brown'. To me these were somewhat awesome - symbols of a world I could not know for some years.

"On Wednesday there were the meetings of the Ladies Aid or The Guild. On Thursday many ladies went out calling on the ladies who had 'Thursdays' engraved on the lower corners of their cards."

At one time there was even a "language" of cards whereby the bending of the corners had special significance.

"Quite apart from such details as the correct size and typography was the difficult symbolism involved in bending the edges. Turning down the upper right-hand corner signified a personal visit; the upper left corner, congratulations; the lower right hand corner, adieu; the lower left corner, condolence; the entire left end, a call on the whole family. This practice, introduced from abroad shortly after the Civil War, commended itself to city dwellers who had little time or inclination for individual visits and yet did not wish to feel negligent of their duties...Despite its conveniences, the custom was becoming passe by the 1890s. The sign language proved too great a tax on the human intelligence." (Reprinted with permission of The MacMillan Company from *LEARNING HOW TO BEHAVE* by Arthur M. Schlesinger. Copyright 1946 by Arthur M. Schlesinger.)

Early card receivers were quite simple, consisting of a small tray about six inches in diameter mounted on a pedestal. And only a few styles were offered.

It was not until the 1870's and 1880's, when homes and home furnishings and styles in clothing reflected the Victorian

No. 158.

Engraved, ... $6.50 (HALYARD).
Engraved, Silver, Gold Inlaid, 7.50 (HASLET).

No. 176.

Silver, . $7.50 (HAMMER).
Gold Lined, 8.50 (HAMPER).

No. 155.

Plain, Gold Lined, . $6.00 (HANDEL).
Coral Chased, . . 6.00 (HANDAL).
Coral Chased, Gold Lined, 6.75 (HANGER).

No. 159.

Silver and Gold Inlaid, $8.00 (HARFOR).

No. 173.

Chased, . $7.50 (HARD).
Niello and Gold, 9.00 (HARDY).

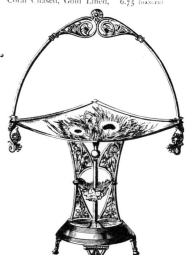

No. 162.

Silver and Gold Inlaid, $7.50 (HARE).

No. 157.

Damascene and Gold Lined, $9.00 (HARMONY).

No. 150.

Chased, . . $9.50 (HARNESS).
Chased, Gold Lined, 10.25 (HARP).

No. 157.

Plain, . $7.25 (HARTON).
Gold Lined, 8.00 (HARLOW).

A page from the Meriden Britannia Company catalog of 1882. The objects shown were offered in several different finishes - silver, gold, engraved, chased, Damascene, Coral chased, and Niello and gold.

110

trend, that card receivers came into their own. The styles then followed and perhaps even exceeded the elaborate and flamboyant taste which was the order of the day.

The old catalogs of the Meriden Britannia Co. of Meriden, Connecticut clearly demonstrate the growing popularity of card receivers, and the increasing variety of sizes, shapes and ornamentation. In 1861, four designs were offered; in 1867—71 there were fourteen; in 1879 the number had increased to thirty-one. The catalog of 1882 offered fifty-three different designs, and that of 1886, fifty-eight. This seems to have been the peak of the elaborate and unusual forms.

And what decorations there were! Card receivers were ornamented with owls, butterflies, children, cherubs, birds, fruits, cats, dogs, flowers and foliage in fantastic arrangements. Many of them included colorful flower vases in what is known today as "art glass."

In the early 1900's, few styles were offered, and by then, most of them were just the card "trays" mentioned by Mrs. Murie in her book.

In addition to the Meriden Britannia Co., other silverware makers in the Meriden, Connecticut area made them too. Such firms as Meriden Silver Plate Co., Middletown Plate Co., Wilcox Silver Plate Co., Wm. Rogers Mfg. Co, Derby Silver Co., and Simpson, Hall, Miller & Co., to name just a few, offered equally attractive assortments.

Despite the widespread custom of leaving cards, and the great variety of card receivers offered by so many makers over a period of forty years, this piece of Victorian silverplate seems to be scarce in antique shops today. One sees them occasionally, but they are not nearly as common as cake baskets, dinner casters, pickle casters, and butter dishes, which flourished in the same period.

Top: Made by Rogers, Smith & Co., Hartford, Conn., between 1856 and 1862. Middle, left: Meriden Silver Plate Co., Meriden, Conn., about 1885; right: Hartford Silver Plate Co., Hartford, Conn., 1884. Bottom, left to right: Meriden Britannia Co., Meriden, Conn., 1873; Meriden Britannia Co., 1882; Derby Silver Co., Derby, Conn., 1883 (inscription on tray reads "Should Owl'd Acquaintance Be Forgot").

This attractive box was made by Meriden Britannia Co. in 1886. Moving the handle back opens the cover and elevates the box.

Cover is raised by drawing on chain. Made by Wilcox S. P. Co., 1884. Height 9¼ inches.

Jewel Caskets

To most people today, the word "casket" has to do with funerals. In fact, one encyclopedia has only one reference under "casket", and this reads, "see funeral customs". Dictionaries, on the other hand, usually give also the definition, "a small chest, as for jewels."

In the early days of the silverplate industry, these little boxes for jewelry were called variously, cases, boxes, and stands but beginning about 1878, the word casket was applied, and this appelation persisted in general use for over twenty years.

At first they were simple in style, typical box shape, and made in only two or three patterns. The piece apparently became a popular one, because each year new designs were cataloged. In a short time, a wide variety was being offered by all the leading makers.

Around 1877, silverware designers, as they did in so many other things, started over-embellishing, not only in the types of ornamentation, but in the shapes as well. Birds, cherubs, cats, lion heads, children, and butterflies were a few of the ornaments applied to the already fancy frames, handles and covers. One casket even had the figure of a little girl on a swing hanging between the overhead handle.

To the fancy ornaments, the designers now added another element, consisting of different types of mechanical gadgets for opening the cover. Many of these were patented, and took the form of chains, gears, rods, and handles which, when pulled or pushed, automatically opened the cover or drawer. Simpson, Hall, Miller and Com-

Unique Jewel Box made by Middletown Plate Co., Middletown, Conn., about 1882. Cover opens by pressing on figure in basket. Height 9½".

pany of Wallingford, Connecticut, in 1887, offered four designs with the comment, "Opening to right or left by patent bail handle."

In shapes, we find such things as acorns, chair, table, sleigh, baby carriage, and old fashioned cradle, to name a few. There were others using colored glass and crystal for the box with gold or silverplated frames. The information about the glass is meager, as usual, but one with a black glass box is described as "Black Fancy, metal mounts, gold and steel finish." Another is called "Decorated Coral Glass," and another "Rose Malachite."

Some of the jewel caskets were quite elaborate, including such things as mirrors, vases and cologne bottles, and were priced as high as thirty-five dollars in 1886. A small simple one cost three dollars, but the average price of most of them was ten to fifteen dollars. Linings were silk, satin, or velvet, in assorted colors.

With the approach of the Twentieth Century, the birds, butterflies, cherubs and unique shapes no longer found favor. And while many containers for jewelry were still being offered, they were made in more conventional forms. The term "casket" also faded from the picture, and in the early 1900s, they were more often called Jewel Boxes.

As might be expected, the Art Nouveau period (1890—1910) had an important influence in this field too, and many boxes were made with that type of decoration.

These fascinating jewel caskets, made between 1877 and 1900, with their unusual forms and fully modeled ornamental figures are not at all common in antique shops today. But they are something worth searching for and collecting.

A handsome casket made by the Derby Silver Co. in 1883. Box is similar to Bristol cased glass, pink outside and white inside. Hand painted floral decorated cover is raised by drawing chain and fastening to a little hook at side. Height 13½".

Top, left: Cover opens when handle is moved back. Made by Wilcox Silver Plate Co. about 1896. Height 10½". Right: The cover of this jewel casket opens like a roll-top desk; as it does, the drawer also opens. Meriden Britannia Co., 1879. Height 9". Bottom, left: Pushing down on the rod opens the cover of this casket made by the Meriden Britannia Co., ca. 1879. Height 7½". Right: Lift-off cover. Made by the Meriden Britannia Co. between 1873 and 1877. Height 8¼".

No. 1162. Gold-lined, . . $7.50.
Meriden S. P. Co., 1879. Height 7".

No. 47. Jewel Table

Half Open.

Meriden Britannia Co., 1879. Height 6".

No. 14, ... $8.00

Meriden Britannia Co., 1877. Length 6".

Decorated glass box and flower vases in silverplated frame by Meriden Britannia Co., 1886. Height 10½".

Cobalt blue translucent glass with hand painted decoration in white. Product of Meriden S. P. Co. about 1880. Height 4½".

Top, left: A handsome box made by the Derby Silver Co., ca. 1896. Hand painted china medallion on cover. Length 5½". Right: Art Nouveau style so popular in the early 1900s. Marked "Victor Silver Co." (a mark used by the Derby Silver Co.). Width 6". Bottom, left: Made by the Middletown Plate Co., ca. 1874. Length 4". Right: Made by Wilcox Silver Plate Co., ca. 1896. Length 4 inches.

Cased glass fruit bowl, lime green inside, plum outside, decorated with enameled flowers in high relief. The silverplated stand was made by the Meriden Britannia Co. in its Hamilton, Ontario, Canada plant, ca. 1895; height 13¾".

Bride's Baskets

In many antique shops today, one of the most attractive and rarest pieces of Victorian silverplate is the bride's basket, or bride's bowl. This is a silverplated frame, or stand, with an insert of elaboratedly formed and decorated glass.

It has been said that this was a favorite gift for the bride-to-be—hence the name. However, at the time they were most popular, those with the overhead handles were simply called fruit bowls, and those on a pedestal without the handle were called fruit stands.

Today these beautiful pieces are highly valued primarily because of the glass but originally the type of glass, or the quality of it, was almost completely ignored. The old catalogs simply say "assorted colors" or "richly decorated glass," or "decorated porcelain," or "canary - ruby lined." But such names as quilted satin glass, cased glass, peach-blow and Mount Washington, which have such significance among collectors of art glass today, were never mentioned.

Later, around 1896, some of the catalog pages say Pomona glass, or Bohemian, but they never elaborated this point, which has now become a most important one.

It was the silverplate manufacturers who introduced these pieces, and they bought the glass part from glass manufacturers. No doubt the glass makers also sold the bowls alone without the silverplated frame or holder.

The glass bowls with the beautiful ruffled or fluted borders are relatively late-comers to the scene. They were first shown in a limited way around 1886, and it was not until the 1890's that they were offered in any quantity or variety. But by that time they seem to have become extremely popular, and were cataloged by all the leading makers of silverplate.

So handsome are these pieces, and so typical of the period, that many fine examples made by such predecessors of International Silver Company as Simpson, Hall, Miller and Company, Meriden Britannia Company, Derby Silver Company, and Wilcox Silver Plate Company can be seen at the famous Corning Museum of Glass in Corning, New York.

Of an earlier vintage were the bowls and stands, and baskets known as berry or preserve dishes. (Also, occasionally, called fruit dishes.) Some of these date back as early as 1861. They differed in that the glass portion was usually cut or engraved crystal or clear pressed glass. A few were offered in tinted pressed glass, but in appearance, these earlier dishes are entirely unlike the elaborate and beautiful "bride's baskets" which came later.

As it did in so many other things, tastes changed. In the early part of the Twentieth Century they were no longer in demand, although a few simple styles were still being offered as late as 1925.

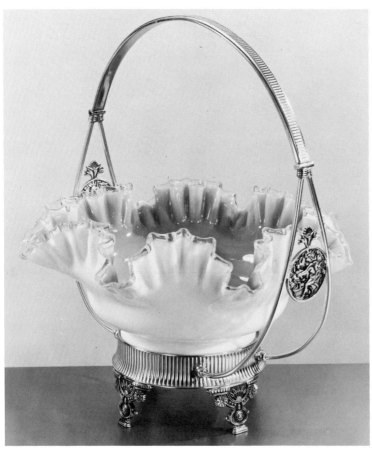

Marked Rogers & Bro. silverplated basket, made about 1890; cased glass bowl with crystal edge, white, pink lined; height 14¾".

Fruit bowl of translucent shaded pink to white glass, applied crystal edge, gold decoration. The silverplated stand was made by the Wilcox Silver Plate Company, in 1886; height 12½".

Left: Silverplated stand marked "Victor Silver Co." (a division of the Derby Silver Co., Derby, Conn.) with shaded white to pink cased glass bowl; multi-colored enamel decoration inside bowl;

8½" high. Right: Shaded blue to white satinglass bowl in a silverplated basket made by the Wm. Rogers Mfg. Co., Hartford, Conn., in 1889; 13" high.

Early silverplated fruit stands. Left: Shown in the 1879 catalog issued by the Meriden Britannia Co.; pressed crystal bowl in the "Tree of Life" pattern; height 10". Right: Cut and engraved crystal bowl atop a stand made by the Meriden Silver Plate Co., before 1879; height 11½".

Left: Wilcox Silver Plate Co. basket, ca. 1896, with cased pink over opal glass bowl decorated with gold leaves and flowers; height 12½". Right: "berry" or "preserve dish" of pressed blue glass in the Daisy and Button pattern; silverplated basket made by the Meriden Britannia Co., ca. 1896; 9" high.

Left to right: Oil lamp offered by Rogers, Smith & Co., in 1882; height 18". A handsome lamp made by the Meriden Britannia Co., ca. 1882; height 20". (Shades on both lamps are close reproductions of the originals.) Boudoir lamp made by the Meriden Silver Plate Co., ca. 1896; height 11½". (This lamp originally had a very fancy shade made of cloth, lace and ribbons.)

Oil Lamps

"Gone with the Wind" lamps, with their handsomely decorated shades and bases, and others with nickel plated, brass, or glass bases (now mostly converted to electricity) are fairly common in antique shops today. But not many people are aware that the silverware makers in the 1880's offered many outstanding lamps with silverplated bases. They seem to be very rare.

In our well lighted homes of today where we can command as much light as we need by simply flicking a switch, it is difficult to visualize how dim must have been the rooms of our forebears once the sun had set.

They had lamps of sorts, to be sure, in the early 1800's, but they were crude affairs at best, burning with an open flame and using whale oil, or grease, as fuel. They gave but little more light than the candles they replaced.

It was not until after 1859 when E. L. Drake drilled the first petroleum well, and the subsequent production of kerosene, that any real improvement in home lighting came about. But from then, until the introduction of gas, and later electricity, the change was a revolutionary one, not only in America, but all over the world.

The glass chimney, which enclosed the flame, was a decided improvement, and it has been written that this "probably was the first lighting improvement in six thousand years."

Many were the improvements in the burners to hold the wicks. Outstanding in this respect was the "Rochester Burner." This employed a circular wick and a central draft principle, which greatly improved the amount of light produced. Meriden, Connecticut became a center for the manufacture of lamps, and the "Rochester" lamp of Edward Miller and Company, introduced in 1884, was one of the earliest lamps to spread the name of Meriden to other lands.

The Meriden Britannia Company, a predecessor of International Silver Company, was producing whale oil and grease lamps in britannia metal as early as 1855. By 1882, apparently aware of the huge market which had opened up by the developments in kerosene burning lamps, they introduced 22 designs. These were offered in a variety of finishes, such as "old or bright copper," "old silver " "old silver, gold inlaid." This "gold inlaid" was simply gold plating some of the parts of the ornamentation.

Shades and globes (glass chimneys) were not included in the price of the lamp, but could be purchased at an "average price of one dollar and twenty-five cents to two dollars and fifty cents net."

In 1886—1887, they offered twenty-nine different styles, including what were called "extension lamps." These stood on the floor and could be raised or lowered.

They, and the other silver makers, did not manufacture the burners, but used the famous Rochester burner, or others apparently made in Meriden. One such burner was marked "B & H," which stood for Bradley and Hubbard, another Meriden lamp maker, founded in 1854, which made thousands of lamps sold throughout the world.

Smaller silverware companies, such as Wilcox Silver Plate Company, and Meriden Silver Plate Company, were also making kerosene lamps. Wilcox shows five designs in their catalog for 1886, and Meriden Silver Plate had four in 1888. Reed and Barton, a large silver maker in Taunton, Massachusetts, offered thirty-two designs in 1885.

When illuminating gas, and eventually electricity took over, the silverware manufacturers largely dropped out of the lamp business. In the early 1900's, they were making some electrified lamps and candlesticks and candelabra, with shades, sometimes called "Electroliers," but by that time, apparently had decided to leave most of the market to those who specialized in the product.

LAMPS, FLUID OR OIL.

No. 128.   No. 127.   No. 126.

GREASE LAMPS.

No. 420.   No. 415.

No. 115.   No. 150.   No. 155.

				Fluid.	Oil.
Fancy Fluted, 7½ inch. high, No. 128,			per dozen,	$7.62½	$7.37
"	7	"	" 127,	"	7.00	6.75
"	5¾	"	" 126,	"	5.87½	5.62
"	6	"	" 115,	"	6.50	6.25
"	6	"	" 150,	"	5.87½	5.62
"	5½	"	" 155,	"	5.50	5.25

No. 410.   No. 405.

Plain, 10 inch. high, No. 420,	.	.	per dozen,	$7.62½
" 8½ " " 415,	.	.	.	"	6.75
" 6½ " " 410,	.	.	"	5.25
" 4 " " 405,	.	.	.	"	3.50

Fluid or oil lamps and grease lamps in Britannia metal illustrated in a Meriden Britannia Co. catalog, ca. 1855.

No. 670. ROCHESTER BURNER.
er and Gold, $27.50 (SPARKING).
Shade extra.

No. 675. ROCHESTER BURNER.
Old Silver, Gold Inlaid, $110.00 (SPARKING).
Height, when extended, 69 inches.
Shade extra.

No. 515.
Enameled Copper Old Silver Mountings, $22.50 (STRAIT)
Shade extra.

(216)

No. 615.
Old Copper, $15.00 (STREAMER).
Old Copper and Old Silver, 17.00 (STRETCHER).

No. 655.
Old Copper, Old Silver Mountings, $100.00 (STRUCTUR).
Height, when extended, 68 inches.

No. 610.
Enameled Copper, Old Silver Mountings, $27.50 (STRICT).
Globe Extra.

(218)

Wilcox Silver Plate Co. Fine Lamps.

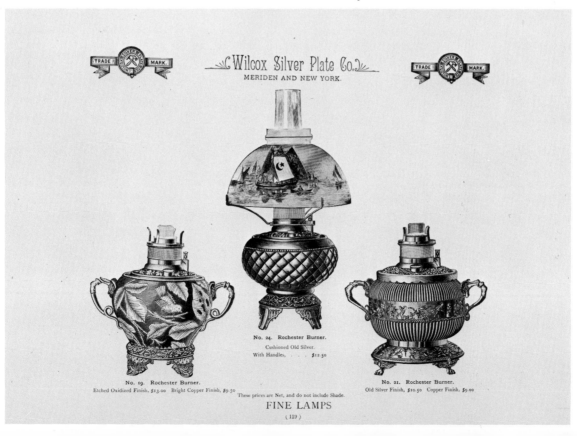

TRADE MARK.   Wilcox Silver Plate Co.   TRADE MARK.
MERIDEN AND NEW YORK.

No. 19. Rochester Burner.
Etched Oxidized Finish, $15.00 Bright Copper Finish, $9.50

No. 24. Rochester Burner.
Cushioned Old Silver.
With Handles, ... $12.50

No. 21. Rochester Burner.
Old Silver Finish, $10.50 Copper Finish, $9.00

These prices are Net, and do not include Shade.

FINE LAMPS

(119)

"Old Silver" table lamps illustrated in a
Meriden Silver Plate Co. catalog, ca. 1888. Height of
each lamp, 16".

No. 2660.

Old Silver, $20.50 (HARMOST).

No. 2658.

Old Silver, $18.25 (HARMEL).

No. 495.

Old or Bright Copper,	$45.00
Old Silver,	50.00
Old Silver, X Gold Inlaid,	56.00
Old Silver, X X Gold Inlaid,	65.00

No. 435.   No. 485.

Table lamps with decorated glass shades and Rochester Burners were illustrated in the Wilcox Silver Plate Co. catalog in 1886. Height of each lamp, approximately 16".

No. 25. Rochester Burner.

Bright Cut Copper Finish, $9.50

No. 20. Rochester Burner.

Old Silver Finish, $9.50   Copper Finish, $8.50

Satin finish, hand engraved, and with applied rose border. Meriden Britannia Co. Ewer 16½" high. Basin 19" diameter.

A product of Simpson, Hall, Miller & Co. Ewer height 15". Basin 18" in diameter.

Lavatory Sets

The convenience of indoor plumbing is, relatively, a recent thing, and the lack of it well within the memory of many persons living today.

The first hotel to install bathrooms and toilets was the Tremont House in Boston, Massachusetts, opened in 1829. It had one hundred and seventy rooms but only eight water closets and eight bathing rooms in the basement to which there was a separate entrance.

As the years went by, eventually water (cold) was piped to rooms, and then hotels could and did advertise "running water in every room." (There is a small sea-side hotel in Connecticut which still so advertises.)

These improvements came first to the cities, but it was many years later that hotels and homes in the smaller towns and outlying areas had such advantages.

So a common piece of furniture in most bedrooms then was the commode, or wash stand as it was sometimes colloquially called. The late Hal Borland, in a fine entertaining book, *"Country Editor's Boy"* (J. B. Lippincott Company) describes a hotel room in a small Colorado town about 1915.

"There were two chairs, one a rocker, two iron beds, and a varnished oak commode. On the commode's white marble top were a big china wash bowl and a matching water pitcher, white with sprigs of red roses. In the cupboard beneath were a big enameled slop pail and two chamber pots sprigged with red roses to match the pitcher and bowl."

Thousands of these wash bowls and pitchers were being sold in china and pottery, and the silverware makers of the period apparently decided that they would like a share of this business.

The Meriden Britannia Company of Meriden, Connecticut, in a modest way as early as 1877, cataloged a plain wash bowl and pitcher in quadruple silverplate for twenty-four dollars. The same style, with an engine-turned design, was priced at thirty dollars.

New designs were added subsequently, so that by 1886, seven styles were current, and many other pieces were added to the sets. A handsome pattern called "Brocade Rose Embossed" included eight pieces: the pitcher, now called a ewer; the wash bowl, now called a basin; plus a brush box, soap box, puff box, sponge dish, cup and covered slop jar, was priced at one hundred and fifty-four dollars and fifty cents. In addition, a satin lined chest or case to hold all these pieces was offered at fifty dollars extra.

The lowly chamber pot was not neglected, and a nine inch covered style was priced at twelve dollars.

But it was not until after the turn of the Century that the Lavatory Sets increased in popularity. From then, until the 1920's when they gradually faded from the picture, most of the silver makers cataloged them. Dozens of different designs were produced, using all the many forms of decoration of the silver craftsman. These included chasing, hand engraving, etching, embossing, engine turning and applied ornaments.

There were some sets in Art Nouveau (eight piece set, one hundred and fourteen dollars) as well as a child's set with smaller ewer and basin priced at sixty-eight dollars and twenty-five cents for eight pieces. Other sets ran as high as two hundred dollars.

Some sets were even larger and included such things as atomizer, cologne bottle, mirror, tooth powder box and tooth brush holder.

The big market, of course, was for those in china, and similar materials. The 1902 catalog of Sears, Roebuck and Company illustrates a ten piece set in "semi-porcelain; shipped from our potteries in Eastern Ohio and Southern Indiana" at only two dollars and twenty cents.

The very best one was "tinted a dark olive green, gently blending towards the center to a soft salmon color, and finally receding to the same rich green at the bottom -

made more attractive by the rich, full gold tracing on all embossed lines."

The ten pieces, bowl, pitcher, covered chamber, covered soap dish, hot water pitcher, brush, vase and mug, sold for five dollars and fifty cents. Adding the large slop jar and cover brought the price to seven dollars and ninety-eight cents.

The weekly pay for wage earners from 1880 through 1920 ranged from fifteen dollars to twenty dollars. So, obviously, these lavatory sets in silverplate were intended only for the more affluent.

It is difficult now to believe that any large market for them existed. Nevertheless, there must have been a substantial market to justify the production of so many designs through some twenty years or more.

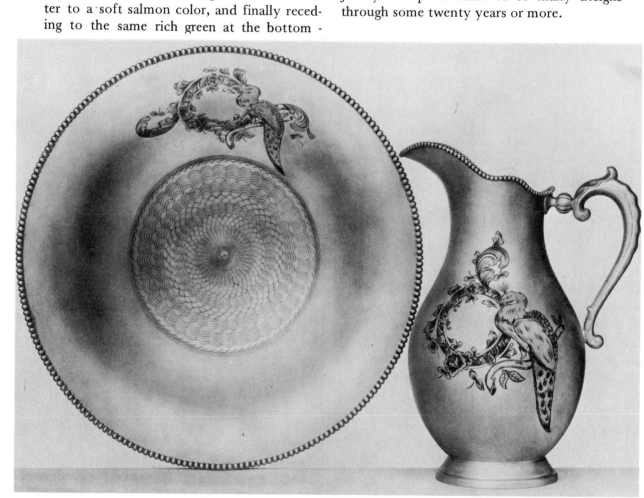

A beaded border and hand engraved peacock decoration, characterized this set by Simpson, Hall, Miller & Co. Basin is 17½" in diameter. Ewer 13½" in height and a capacity of 5 pints.

Another offering of the Meriden Britannia Co. Ornamentation is embossed. Ewer is 17" tall. Eight pieces in silverplate priced at $125.00, but also offered with parts of the ornaments gold plated (called gold inlaid) at $158.00.

Satin engraved Lavatory Set by Meriden Britannia Company includes ewer (pitcher), basin, soap box, brush box, puff box, tooth powder box, sponge dish, cup (gold lined), atomizer, cologne bottle and mirror. Originally priced at $131.50. Ewer 18" tall.

Hand engraved set in the Art Nouveau style by Meriden Silver Plate Co. Height of ewer 18½".

Child's set. Satin finish, hand engraved. Ewer about 14" high. Eight piece set priced at $68.25. Made by Meriden Britannia Co.

*Wilcox Silver Plate Company made this
Lavatory Set with applied decorations in the Art
Nouveau style. Ewer 16" tall; basin 17" in diameter.*

Left: Toilet stand with ring drawer by Meriden Silver Plate Co., 1879. Height 15". Right: One of the simpler styles by Meriden Britannia Co. in the 1870s. Height 10½".

Toilet Stands

The market for silverware has always been considered a feminine one, primarily. True enough, there were many things made for family use, such as tea sets, butter dishes, dinner casters, pickle casters, and other dining accessories. Some things were made for children, such as child's cups and plates, child size knives, forks, and spoons. And there were a few things for men, such as mustache cups, shaving mugs and stands, smoking sets, cigar boxes, and humidors.

However, it was the lady (or ladies) of the house who received the most attention, and of the many things made to appeal to them, by far the greater number seems to have been those concerned with milady's dressing table.

There were combs, brushes and mirrors, countless boxes for gloves, handkerchiefs, soap, hair pins and jewels. There were curling irons, hair receivers, powder puff containers, and hat pin holders, to name only a few.

One of the most unusual pieces was the toilet stand (or toilet set, as it was sometimes called.) The simplest of these was a silverplated frame to hold a single bottle of cologne or toilet water. The elaborate styles many times held two bottles, a puff box, a vase for flowers, and a drawer for jewelry or comb and brush.

As was the case with the beautiful bride's baskets, very little is said about the handsome decorated glass bottles and vases.

A catalog for 1871 states, "The bottles in these sets are of the latest Paris pattern and will be changed as often as new patterns are received."

Another calls the bottles "Malachite-blue, pink, white or canary." And another, simply, "Aqua Marine decorated." But in most cases, the glass is not mentioned.

These toilet stands seem to have started in a modest way about 1867, but by 1877, must have increased in popularity. By July of that year, the Meriden Britannia Company, was offering forty-one different designs. In September of 1878, they added eighteen new styles, and by September 1879, an additional thirty-nine.

Their catalog for 1882 illustrated seventy-one styles, and for 1886 the variety reached eighty-five different designs. They ranged in price from two dollars for a tiny stand holding a two ounce bottle to seventy-five dollars for the most elaborate. This fancy affair had bottles for cologne, the puff box, a mirror, and female figures with candle holders for six candles perched on their heads. The stand was decorated in gold.

As it did in so many other cases, the demand diminished. By 1890, only a few were being offered, and by the turn of the Century, the silver makers apparently stopped making them.

But between 1877 and 1890, a great many must have been made. It seems reasonable to assume that the makers would not have offered such a wide variety unless there was an active market for them.

The single bottle styles occasionally show up in antique shops today, but the elaborate styles appear to be non-existent.

The Middletown Plate Company. Toilet Sets.

"No. 3, Antique" toilet set made by the Meriden Britannia Co., ca. 1867. The white opaline bottles have been given an acid (matt) finish and decorated with Grecian figures in rust, black and buff. Height 9".

No. 152. With Jewel Drawer.
Silver,   .   .   . $20.00 (HOUND).
Silver, Gold Inlaid,   22.00 (HOUSE)

No. 151.
Silver,   .   . $17.00 (HOVER).
Silver, Gold Inlaid, 19.00 (HUB).

No. 178.
Silver,   . $26.50 (HUDDLE)
Silver, Gold Inlaid,   29.00 (HUE).

No. 124.
X X Coral Rose, .   . $33.00 (HOVERING).
Gold and Steel Finish,   36.00 (HUFF).

No. 131.
(Same style, with Bottles like No. 173.)
Silver,   . $24.00 (HUGE).

*Meriden Britannia Co. catalog of 1882.
Height (right) 16½".*

No. 68. Gold and Silver Finish, ... $38.00

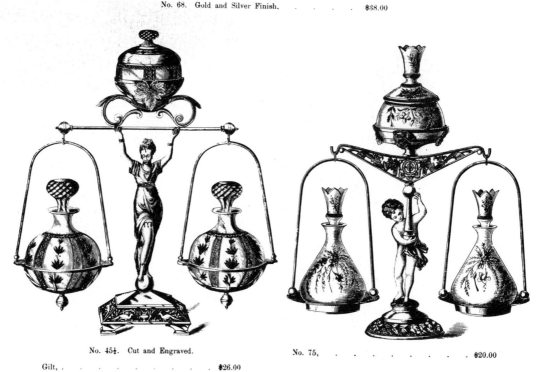

No. 45½. Cut and Engraved.

Gilt, ... $26.00

No. 75, ... $20.00

(121)

Meriden Britannia Co. catalog of 1877.
Heights approximately 16½".

No. 200. Toilet.

Silver, . . $60.00 (INCOGNITO).

Silver, Gold Inlaid, 75.00 (INCOME).

No. 152. With Jewel Drawer.

Silver, . . . $20.00 (HOUND).

Silver, Gold Inlaid, . 22.00 (HOUSE).

No. 211.

Silver, ... $30.00 (MORTISE).

Silver, Gold Inlaid, . 35.00 (MOSLEM).

(350)

Meriden Britannia Co. catalog of 1886.
Height (top) 22", (bottom) 13½–14".

*A product of Meriden Britannia Co. about
1900. Mirror is 9½" long.*

Toilet Ware

It has been said many times that two things one can be sure of in this world are death and taxes. To these one might properly add another, and that is — change.

To the pewter and silverware makers change was no stranger. They experienced the change from pewter to britannia ware, from coin silver to sterling and after 1847, the tremendous change to electro-silverplate which influenced the sterling market, but more importantly, put pewter products into limbo for years to come.

As important as these changes were, equally important were the changes in tastes, in fashions and in life-styles which seriously affected the popularity and consequently the demand for certain articles. Such things as silverplated ice pitchers, dinner casters, figural napkin rings, card receivers, cake baskets, fruit baskets and stands, nut bowls, pickle casters and butter dishes, which were the "bread and butter" part of the silverplated holloware business, had largely passed out of the picture by the first quarter of the Twentieth Century.

Some of the slack, of course, was taken up by increased popularity of other products and one of these, which in its turn also took the count, was dresserware, or as it was usually called - toiletware.

For ladies the basic set consisted of comb, hairbrush and hand mirror - for gentlemen, a comb and two military brushes.

But that was only the beginning. For the ladies in many designs, a complete matching set could include as many as twenty pieces. This would consist of comb, brush, mirror, cloth brush, velvet brush, hat brush, puff box, whisk broom, hat pin holder, jewel box, pin tray, hair pin box and hair receiver, plus manicure pieces - nail polisher, nail file, cuticle knife, corn knife, shoehorn, button hook and cream box.

For gentlemen, a set consisting of two military brushes, a cloth brush and a hat brush was called a "Navy Set" and could be bought for twelve dollars and twenty-five cents. Matching pieces included such things as shaving mug and brush, soap box, whisk broom and collar-button box.

Children were not neglected. Small-size sets were made, and American Silverplate Company offered a six-piece set, hand etched with pictures from Peter Pan described as "The True Story of Peter Pan Told in Silverplate." It was discontinued in 1924 and at that time priced at seventeen dollars and twenty-five cents. Three-piece basic sets for both ladies and gentlemen ranged in price from seven dollars and seventy-five cents to sixteen dollars and fifty cents.

Toiletware in silverplate is now a thing of the past. It's popularity lasted about thirty-five years.

Among the predecessors of International Silver Company, combs, brushes and mirrors had been offered, in a limited way, as early as the 1800's but it was not until after 1900 that toiletware increased in popularity and produced significant dollars in sales.

Around 1894-1896, certain of these predecessors established secondary trademarks for less expensive silverplate and, under these marks as well as their major trademarks, produced literally hundreds of different designs in toiletware. Many beautiful patterns were offered, employing all of the various techniques for ornamentation such as hand chasing, hand engraving, embossing, hand etching and engine turning.

The secondary trademarks and the companies that used them were:

Major Brand	Secondary Brand
Derby Silver Company	Victor Silver Company
Meriden Britannia Company	Forbes Silver Company
Meriden Silverplate Company	Eureka Silver Company
Simpson, Hall, Miller and Company	American Silverplate Company
Middletown Plate Company	Superior Silver Company
Wilcox Silverplate Company	Superior Silver (Plate) Company

Art nouveau designs were widely used, and in this field the Derby Silver Company seems to have excelled. Under both the Derby and Victor trademarks, they offered more than twenty-five designs with such names as "Love's Message", "The Blue Bells", "Shower of Roses", "The Peerless", "The Cupid", "The Birth of the Rose", "The Orchid Girl", "The Marguerite", "Joy of Dawn", "Cupid's Courtship", "Pansy", "Iris", Daffodil" and "Orchid".

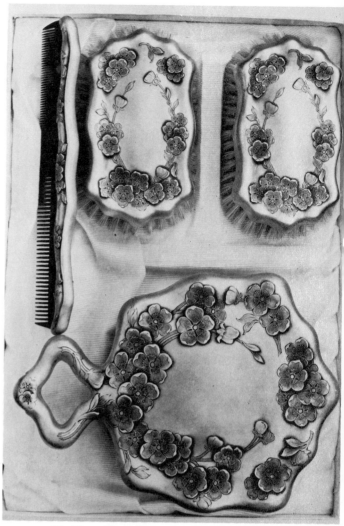

Meriden Silver Plate Co. made this gentle-men's set under the Eureka Silver Co. mark about 1920. Four pieces, in a white satin-lined case, were a pair of military brushes, comb and ring mirror.

Toilet and Manicure combination in "Loves Message" made under Victor Silver Co. trademark. Twelve pieces for $29.00.

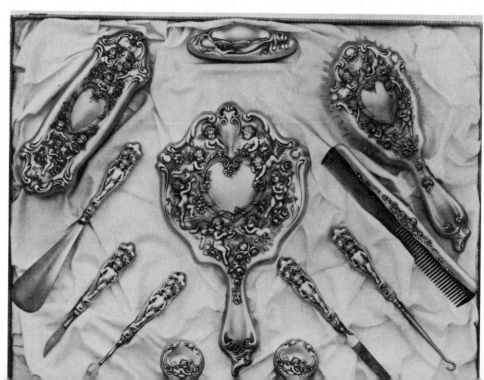

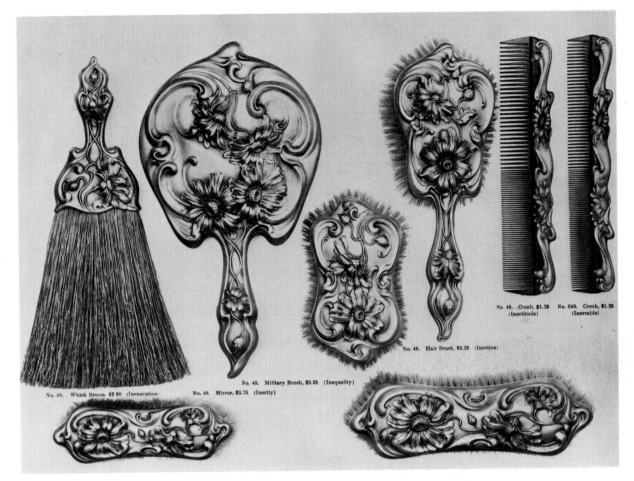

No. 48. Whisk Broom, $2.50 (Inexecution)   No. 48. Mirror, $3.75 (Inertly)   No. 48. Military Brush, $3.25 (Inequality)   No. 48. Hair Brush, $3.25 (Insertion)   No. 48. Comb, $1.25 (Inertitude)   No. 048. Comb, $1.25 (Inerrable)

Ladies' and gentlemens' eight piece set consisting of whisk broom, mirror, man's military brush, lady's comb, man's comb, hat brush and cloth brush. Pattern is "The Marguerite" by Derby Silver Co. about 1904.

Infant's toilet set with etched Peter Pan decorations. Set consists of soap box, puff box, comb, hair brush, mirror and fine tooth comb. Mirror 6¾".

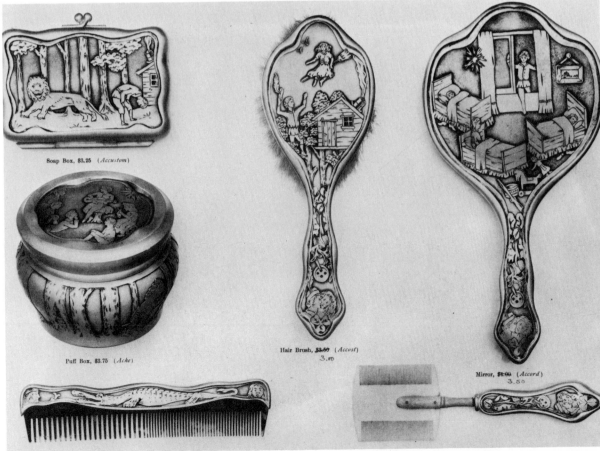

Soap Box, $3.25 (Accustom)

Puff Box, $3.75 (Ache)

Hair Brush, $3.60 (Accost)
3.00

Mirror, $3.00 (Accord)
3.50

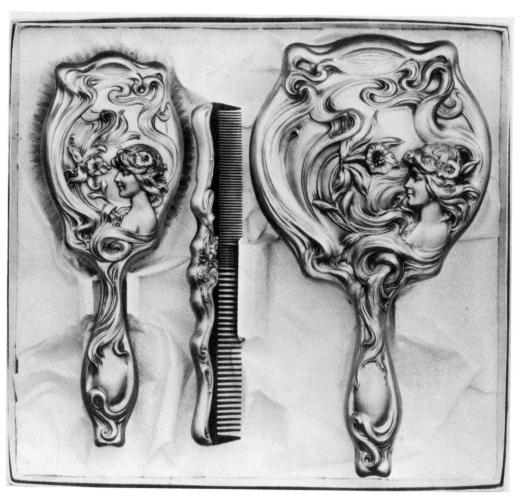

Derby Silver Co.'s "The Orchid Girl." Three pieces retailed for $8.25. About 1912.

Victor Silver Co. Three piece set in "The Cupid" pattern.

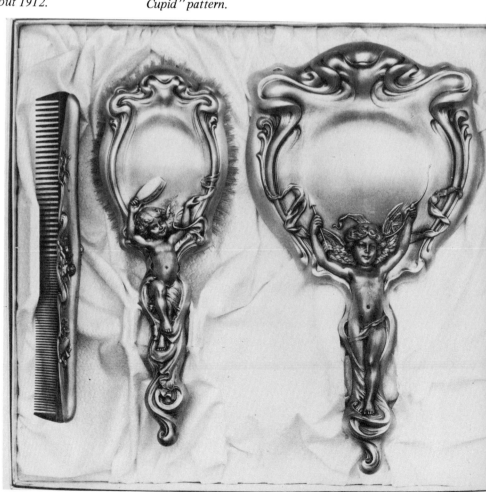

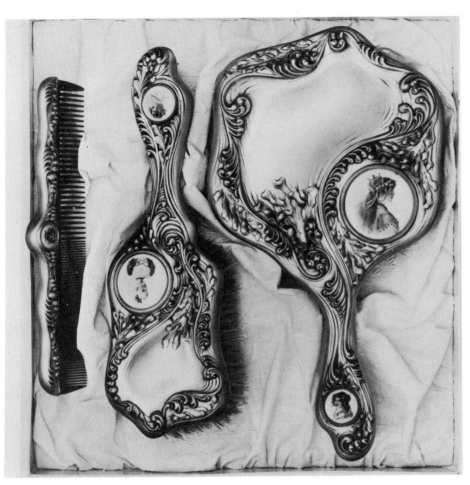

Comb, brush and mirror set mounted with colored porcelain miniatures. American Silver Plate Co. trademark. About 1915.

"Love's Message" by Derby Silver Plate Co. about 1916. Mirror 10" long.

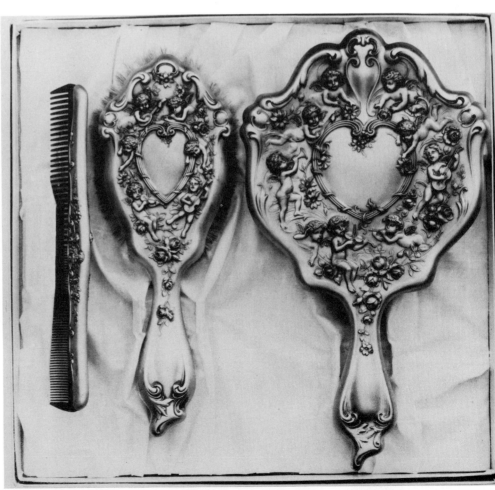

Ashbil Griswold from a portrait painted in 1846.

Beaker and soap box. The "touch-mark" on these two pieces is just the letters A. G. in a rectangle. Beaker 3" high; soap box 4½" in diameter. A similar soap box by Griswold is on display at the Smithsonian Institution in Washington, D. C.

Ashbil Griswold

Over 200 years ago the first tinware made in America was produced in Berlin, Connecticut. This industry soon spread to adjoining towns and as early as 1770 historical records show many tin makers located in Meriden, some ten miles south of Berlin.

These tin products were distributed almost exclusively by peddlers, called Yankee peddlers or tin peddlers and they carried on their wagons, in addition to tin, such things as pewter spoons, steel knives with bone or ivory handles, plates, pots and other pieces of pewter and a wide variety of what were called Yankee notions. By 1789 the wagon peddlers, making Meriden their source of supply, began to appear and were much in evidence.

In Rocky Hill, Connecticut, Captain Thomas Danforth, one of five generations of pewter makers, carried on a successful business and under his supervision many young men learned their trade. Among them were Charles and Hiram Yale, originally from Meriden but later establishing their own business in Wallingford, Connecticut. Another was Ashbil Griswold, born in Rocky Hill, April 4, 1784. Following the completion of his apprenticeship with Danforth he came to Meriden in 1808 and started his own factory, making pewter spoons, dishes, pots and other smaller pieces which could easily be cast. (The common method in those days.) It is reported that he ate his first meal and boarded in the home of James Frary in the north part of the town. This section was referred to in those days as Clarksville (later. Fraryville). In 1810 he married Frary's daughter, Lucy.

Land records show that on November 7, 1808 he bought land from Ira Yale, just north of Yale's house, "with a shop standing thereon about nine rods and one rod in width on northwest and south of said shop." In 1810 he built a house which still stands today although now much changed in appearance through alterations.

Fortunately, from a series of account books now preserved in the Historical Library of International Silver Company, a tremendous amount of information can be gleaned about Ashbil Griswold's business and the business of those who followed him. These account books were uncovered about forty-two years ago in the attic of the former home of William W. Lyman.

Griswold's first products according to his original account books for 1808 were basins in the gallon, half-gallon and pint sizes, dippers, large and small, and plates. By the latter part of the year he was selling spoons at fifty cents a dozen, small tablespoons at eighty-seven and one-half cents a dozen. The following year shows charges for porringers, coat buttons and large soup ladles. In 1809 his pewter button sales through the peddlers were very large, some of them buying twenty-five or even fifty gross at a time. But it appears that by 1817 more people were casting buttons and in that year Griswold recorded a sale of "one pair of button molds at ten dollars" and from then on apparently concentrated on his regular line of pots, spoons, plates, etc.

By 1825 he was making varying grades of his wares such as "best" pots at ninety-five cents to one dollar and ten cents each.

Griswold pewter and account books. The first few pages of the small "Day-Book" in the foreground record transactions with accounts in Baltimore as early as 1807 (presumeably while he was still with Danforth).

Griswold pewter sugar bowl; 5½" high.

An unexplained mystery occurs on September 1, 1808, when, beginning then and continuing to October 1809 Griswold's transactions are recorded in English money - pounds, shillings and pence. Prior to and following that period of just a year, accounts are figured in dollars and cents.

Because most of Griswold's products were distributed through peddlers and because cash was scarce, a great part of the business was carried on through barter. Griswold equipped his peddlers with pewter of course (and financed them too), plus things taken in trade and also with other Meriden-made products such as combs and buttons. There were combs of brass, horn and ivory and buttons of bone, horn, wood, ivory and glass. There were also large quantities of tinware made in the area. These were paid for, sometimes in cash, but more often in Griswold products. The year 1838 records transactions with George Mitchell who supplied brass combs and took in trade "best teapots." Noah Pomeroy supplied tinware taking Griswold's tea pots. William Little furnished thirty-seven gross of buttons and was paid in pewter spoons.

The variety of goods the peddlers took in exchange is almost unbelievable, so that Griswold either by choice or by force of circumstances practically became a "general merchant" in addition to being a pewter maker. The records show such things as muskrat, otter, fox and mink skins, shoes, goose, duck and hen's feathers in large quantities. (There is one record of 3,088 pounds and another for 2,330 pounds.) Also old metal, sheeting, cashmere, broadcloth, white rags, common rags, cotton and silk thread, satinette, wood faucets, cigars, gun powder, molasses, wine, rum, brandy and whiskey, wool, British oil, peppermint, quills and other things too numerous to list.

In 1831 there is a record that on June 22 Griswold sent four hundred and thirty-one and one-half pounds of beeswax to New York to R. K. Clark "to sell for me." Clark in turn bought Griswold's merchandise.

One notation made in March of 1823 shows that Curtis and Upson (peddlers) returns included among other things over four hundred yards of cloth of various kinds and for which they were credited one hundred and sixty-seven dollars and sixty cents.

In November 1824 they brought in over eight hundred yards of textiles valued at one hundred and seventy-eight dollars and took out pewter pots, spoons and buttons, combs of ivory, horn and wood, tinware, coffee mills, faucets, Spanish and common cigars and five hundred and sixty-five pounds of feathers.

There was a more or less regular schedule of value for these things. For example, hen's feathers - seven to ten cents a pound, goose feathers - forty to forty-eight cents a pound, mink skins - twenty-five to thirty-two cents each, fox - fifty-five to one dollar and twelve cents each, quills - twenty-eight cents per one hundred, sheeting seventeen to twenty-three cents per yard, cotton cloth - twelve to sixteen cents yard, old pewter - sixteen to eighteen cents pound, cotton thread - one-half cent skein, silk thread - three cents skein, wool yarn - six cents skein, beeswax - thirty-two to thirty-four cents pound, maple sugar - eight cents pound, brandy - forty cents gallon, rum - seventy-five to eighty-seven and one-half cents gallon, whiskey - twenty-five cents gallon. Spanish cigars - one dollar and fifty cents to two dollars box, common cigars - twenty-five to thirty-seven and one-half cents a box.

Among the names of peddlers most often mentioned are:

Curtis and Upson (1822 - 1825 - 1831)
Chester and Halsey Rice (1824 - 1830)
Asahel Curtis (1823)
Benjamin Upson (1825)

An interesting fact which turns up is the matter of "bad" money. In 1823 the peddlers, Chester and Halsey Rice, returned some cash which was charged back to them as "Eagle money, New Haven, bad, $34.00" and "State Bank, Taunton, money bad -

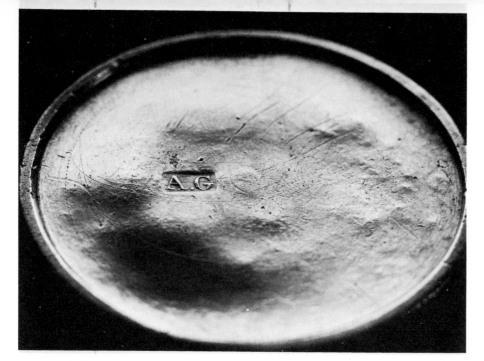

This mark of Griswold's (enlarged) was used primarily on small articles like beakers, soap boxes, etc.

Most commonly used marks by Griswold (enlarged). On tea and coffee pots these were sometimes stamped on the <u>inside</u> bottom of the pot.

$2.00." Banks in those days issued their own money and were frequently unstable. Sometimes they were able to honor their paper money at face value; other times no one would take it at a discount of half or more.

In 1833 Ashbil Griswold was one of the founders and first president of the first bank organized in Meriden. He served in that capacity for four years. In his account book on October 29 he makes this charge - "Meriden Bank, dr. postage six cents, junk bottle for ink ten cents, postage thirty-five cents, 3/4 cord wood three dollars and fifty-six cents, cartage on iron chest thirty-seven and one-half cents." (A most meticulous man.)

In addition to being a bank president, equipping and financing peddlers, and making pewter, Ashbil Griswold made a practice of letting various individuals use his wagons. Most people apparently had their own horses because the usual charges in the account books are for wagon rental only. These were to Berlin, Connecticut - twenty-five cents; Hartford - sixty-five cents; New Haven - seventy-five cents; Waterbury - sixty cents; Westfield - thirty cents. In 1837 James Frary was credited with twelve gross knobs at one dollar per gross; two dozen lamps at six dollars to apply on "horse trade."

Perhaps because of these added duties, about this time Griswold seems to have given more responsibility to Ira Couch who had been working for him for a number of years and in 1834 made him a partner. The firm then became known as Griswold and Couch.

That Griswold was doing a thriving business may be surmised from the account book for 1838 when on July 1 Couch took nine hundred and twenty-five dollars to New York to buy stock. He made a similar trip, with one thousand, one hundred and fifty dollars on October 19.

Ten years earlier, in 1828, there is a record of one shipment of tin which Griswold bought in New York. It weighed three thousand, eight hundred and fifty pounds and since there was no railroad it came by boat up the Connecticut River to Middletown, Connecticut, thence by horse and cart overland some ten miles to Meriden.

By 1843, Griswold apparently decided to be less active and there is evidence that he and Couch were going out of business under that firm name. Records show the sale of some of the manufacturing equipment to James A. Frary. However, he continued in a minor way and as late as 1847 was selling Frary metal supplies and pot tips (finials) at ten cents per hundred and moulds at twelve and one-half cents each. From 1848 to 1851 Lyman was evidently occupying a shop owned by Griswold who made frequent charges for work and repairs on the building, insurance and other items.

There were other pewter makers in the Meriden area and Griswold did business with them, too, in the 1820's. In the 1830's as Griswold and Couch, there are numerous charges to such makers as James A. Frary, I. C. Lewis, W. W. Lyman, L. J. Curtis and later still, H. C. Wilcox. For example, in 1838 they were furnishing Frary with antimony and in 1839 sold Banka tin to Lewis and Curtis. In 1834 they supplied Josiah Danforth with pigs of tin and with tea pot tips.

W. W. Lyman came as an apprentice to Griswold and Couch in 1836 and in 1844 went into business for himself taking Ira Couch as partner. This was a brief relationship. Lyman bought his partner's interest and Couch died in 1845 at the age of 42.

On September 6, 1844 Lyman married Roxanna G. Frary, daughter of James A. Frary and adopted daughter of Ashbil Griswold. (According to Griswold's will.) No explanation is given as to why she was adopted.

In addition to all his other activities, Ashbil Griswold was a representative in the Connecticut State Legislature in 1820, 1826, 1828, 1831 and again in 1847.

He was an active member of Saint Andrews Church and served variously as vestryman, parish clerk, delegate to conventions and member of a building committee through the years from 1822 to 1839. In

A grouping of Ashbil Griswold pewter.

Teapot by Griswold. Height 6½".

1847 he was a member of the building committee when a new church was erected.

His first wife, Lucy, daughter of James Frary, died December 12, 1835. His second wife was Ann (Hall) Lyman, widow of Andrew Lyman, who was a brother of W. W. Lyman. She died October 25, 1870.

Griswold, himself, may not have been directly involved in the organization of Meriden Britannia Company in 1852. He died March 30, 1853, but the men who carried on the business of making pewter and britannia wares, W. W. Lyman and James H. Frary, and who were associated with him, in both a business and family way, were. Others with whom he did business, Lemuel J. Curtis, Isaac C. Lewis and Horace C. and Dennis C. Wilcox were among the founders also.

The account books from which much of this information was obtained were discovered in the attic of the former home of William W. Lyman, about forty-seven years after his (Lyman's) death.

The following years were to see vast changes as the new process of electro-silver-plating advanced and the britannia makers started to silverplate their britannia products. Ashbil Griswold was evidently an honored and respected man in his community and certainly a powerful influence in the establishment and growth of the pewter and britannia industry out of which came the Meriden Britannia Company.

W. W. Lyman.

Mrs. W. W. Lyman, adopted dauthter of
Ashbil Griswold.

W. W. Lyman

A name seldom seen today in relation to antique britannia ware, early silverplate and other products is that of W. W. Lyman. Yet this man made significant contributions to those industries in his day, as well as to the business, social and political life in his chosen town of Meriden, Connecticut.

William Worcester Lyman was born in Woodruff, Vermont, March 29, 1821. When he was but seven years old his father died and with his mother the boy moved to Northford, Connecticut.

In 1836 he came to Meriden and served a five year apprenticeship in the shop of Griswold and Couch, britannia makers. This business had been founded in 1808 by Ashbil Griswold, Meriden's first pewter maker.

In 1844 he went in business for himself, making cast britannia spoons, coffee and teapots, etc., taking as a partner, Ira Couch. A short time later he bought his partner's interest and continued on his own in the old Frary shop which was owned by Griswold. Griswold's account book shows charges against Lyman for two years' insurance on the shop - five dollars; also other charges over the next two or three years including "work on a system and the necessary pump and pipes."

At this time these small manufacturers bought and sold to each other and the records show numerous transactions of this kind. Griswold, for example, in addition to making his own finished products sold "moulds at twelve and one-half cents each" and "nine hundred pot tips at ten cents per hundred."

It was a period of many short term partnerships and Lyman was a participant in several of them. Early in 1841 he had as a partner another britannia maker, Lemuel J. Curtis, under the name of Curtis and Lyman. For two years his partner was I. C. Lewis and by 1852, back again with Curtis, the firm was known as W. W. Lyman and Company.

At the time of his death, he was one of the directors and largest stockholders of the Meriden Britannia Company. He was also, until 1878, president of the Meriden Cutlery Company, one of the prime movers of the street railway and a director in the Meriden Horse Railway Company. He was a director of two local banks and the first president of the Meriden Flint Glass Company.

Mr. Lyman also served Meriden in the state legislature in 1849, 1881 and 1882 was a member of the Common Council in his town and active in the affairs of his church.

H. C. Wilcox and Company

Two enterprising Yankee peddlers, Horace C. Wilcox and his brother, Dennis C. Wilcox, under the name of H. C. Wilcox and Company had for sometime been marketing most of the products of Meriden's small but growing britannia ware factories. These included I. C. Lewis and Company, L. J.

Curtis, James S. Frary and Company, John Munson of Wallingford, and, of course, W. W. Lyman and Company.

From old account books preserved in the Historical Library of International Silver Company we learn that during 1847 Lyman sold H. C. Wilcox and Company pots and other items to the tune of $2,267.13.

Although the prices of tea and coffee pots varied according to size and style, many transactions are recorded at prices ranging from seven dollars and fifty cents to twelve dollars and fifty cents per dozen.

An "account book" covering the period from May 10, 1852 to the final closing of the W. W. Lyman and Company business in June of 1853 shows charges to some forty-six individuals or companies.

In addition to the usual tea and coffee pots, Lyman supplied covered pitchers in three sizes at nine dollars to twenty dollars a dozen, sugars and creams at five dollars a dozen, spittoons seven dollars a dozen, casters nine dollars a dozen, ladles one dollar and seventy-five cents a dozen, three styles of fluid lamps from three dollars and fifty cents to four dollars and twenty-five cents a dozen, fluid bed lamps one dollar and sixty-two cents a dozen and fluid swing lamps at seven dollars a dozen. Pint mugs were three dollars and twenty-five cents a dozen, goblets without handles one dollar, with handles one dollar and twelve cents a half dozen, dish candlesticks two dollars and twenty-five cents and others at three dollars and fifty cents a dozen. There was something called a lemonade mixer priced at two dollars and fifty cents and three dollars and fifty cents a dozen.

In 1830 wages were from seventy-five cents to one dollar per day; in the 1840's one dollar to one dollar and fifty cents per day and in 1852 about two dollars per day was earned by the most skillful workers.

Metals used for making pewter and britannia were, in 1830, priced as follows per pound -- zinc five cents, antimony twenty-three cents, lead five cents copper seventeen cents and tin, the main ingredient, also seventeen cents.

By 1895, zinc and copper had only increased in price by one cent, antimony and lead actually decreased but tin jumped to thirty cents a pound.

The Wilcox brothers were convinced that more opportunities would be offered if all these small suppliers were consolidated and so in December 1852 they organized the Meriden Britannia Company with a capital stock of fifty thousand dollars.

The subscribers were, in addition to the Wilcoxes, I. C. Lewis, James A. Frary, L. J. Curtis, John Munson and W. W. Lyman. Others involved were George R. Curtis, and Samuel Simpson. The first president was I. C. Lewis.

The Meriden Britannia Works; the building on the left is the first factory built around 1856; on the right is the building put up in 1863.

The dominating group behind Meriden Britannia Co. about 1855–1860. Back row, left to right: H. C. Wilcox, I. C. Lewis, George R. Curtis, D. C. Wilcox. Front row: John Munson, L. J. Curtis, Samuel Simpson, W. W. Lyman (W. H. Johnson).
W. H. Johnson was not one of the founders. He worked for Meriden Britannia in that very first office beginning in October, 1853, at the age of 14.
He apparently was an energetic and resourceful youth and was looked upon with favor by the Wilcox brothers.
In 1861, he enlisted in the Army and was shortly promoted to First Sargeant and later Second Lieutenant in Company K, Connecticut Volunteers.
He died in the war on April 6, 1862.
Perhaps because he was so well liked by the officers of the Meriden Britannia Company he was included in the group photograph.

Meriden Britannia Co's Works, Conn. U.S.

The Lyman Fruit Jar

After the Meriden Britannia Company was formed, Mr. Lyman devoted less time to that part of the business and turned more to other interests. His aptness for inventions came to the fore and on August 30, 1858 he was granted a patent (Number 21348) for an "Improved Method of Sealing Preserve Cans."

On December 28 of that same year another patent (Number 22436) was granted for "Improvement in Fruit Cans." This was an especially molded glass jar of unique construction with a metal cap providing a means of effecting an air tight seal.

He spent thousands of dollars developing this jar which was called the Lyman Fruit Jar and was widely heralded as the first jar of that character ever produced.

No record has been found as to who made the glass jars but the Meriden Britannia Company, not averse to turning an honest dollar, undertook to handle the selling of them. Records exist showing that in the latter part of 1863 sales totalled $32,408 and for the entire year of 1864 a total of $251,319 at list prices.

This covered 1,952 gross of the pint size at twenty-four dollars a gross; 5,600 gross quarts at thirty dollars per gross and 1,232 half gallons at thirty-eight dollars per gross.

Another jar called the Lyman Fruit Jar was covered by patent Number 41575 dated February 9, 1864 issued to Elbridge Harris of Boston and assigned to W. W. Lyman. It claimed "forming a groove or depression in or around the neck of the vessel, for the retention of an elastic ring or bank impervious to air."

The Lyman Jars were popular during the 1860's and '70's and were eventually sold to the Hero Fruit Jar Company of Philadelphia.

Lyman Fruit Jars. Covered by Patent No. 41575, Feb. 9, 1864 and re-issued Jan. 22, 1867.

Improvements in the Manufacture of Tea and Coffee Pots

Another patent to the credit of Mr. Lyman was granted October 15, 1867 (Number 69922) titled as above. It describes a method of locking a hard metal bottom, such as copper, to the britannia metal tea and coffee pots through the use of the manufacturing process known as "spinning." The method of doing so is described.

It might be supposed that this improvement was for the purpose of preventing the bottom from melting when placed on a hot surface as would be the case with plain britannia.

While this was probably a correlative benefit, the true purpose as expressed in the patent papers was, "There is less liability of melting the body in the process of soldering, the soldering can be prosecuted with greater rapidity, and with less liability of melting the britannia body, and it is also believed that a good joint can be produced without soldering. They may, therefore, be united with or without solder. Thus, a cheaper, better, and more desirable article is produced thereby."

This invention also serves to substantiate the fact that by 1867 the technique of spinning was an established method of manufacturing (as opposed to the casting which was employed in the making of the much earlier pewter).

Improved Refrigerating Pitcher

Patent Number 20499, dated June 8, 1858, covers this pitcher which was actually what was commonly called an Ice Pitcher. This was an extremely popular item constructed with a double wall and first patented by James Stimpson of Baltimore, October 17, 1854.

The main feature of Lyman's improvement was the "valve" and the location of it which he described thusly. "I make no claim to a valve in the end of the nozzle or on the lid of the pitcher, as valves have heretofore been placed there. Nor do I claim a single valve located anywhere. But I claim, in the manufacture of ice pitchers, the particular location of the valve, viz. in the throat of the nozzle, when said valve shuts into instead of against the opening and is constructed with double sides, or made hollow, provided with a projection lip or shoulder, and having its seat provided with a projection lip or shoulder."

This valve was featured in Meriden Britannia's catalogs of 1861 and 1867 with the statement - "Placed in the throat of the nozzle to all our ice pitchers" and it was used for many years.

Some of the ice pitchers found in antique shops today include this feature and are stamped on the bottom with the appropriate patent designation.

William Worcester Lyman died a wealthy man in Meriden on November 15, 1891 at the age of seventy. He was still a director of the Meriden Britannia Company and held directorships in eight other enterprises in the area.

The large Victorian home he built on Britannia Street still stands. It is but a step from Griswold Street where the original Ashbil Griswold factory stood and where he learned his trade and only a short distance from the old Frary Shop location he later occupied. It was also close by the Meriden Flint Glass Company of which he was president.

LYMAN'S PATENT DOUBLE VALVE.

William Rogers, from a miniature painted on ivory about 1831.

The Rogers Brothers

Coin Silver Period

For over one hundred and thirty years the name Rogers has been synonymous with silverware, attributable entirely to three Rogers brothers, William, Asa and Simeon of Hartford, Connecticut.

They were sons of a farmer located on the Windsor Road, Hartford and decendants of James Rogers who came from England to what is now New London, Connecticut in 1635.

The Rogers brothers' fame was built during the age of electro silverplate but what is not generally known is that all three brothers were experienced silversmiths when coin silver spoons were made largely by hand and long before electroplate became popular after 1847.

William was born in 1801, Asa in 1806 and Simeon in 1812.

With the growth of industry in Connecticut it was not unusual for farm boys, like the Rogers, to start learning a trade and records show that in 1820, William, now nineteen years old, was apprenticed to Joseph Church, a jeweler and gold and silversmith, doing business on Ferry Street in Hartford.

Five years later, having served his apprenticeship, William was admitted to the firm and an announcement to this effect was published in the *HARTFORD COURANT* December 6, 1825.

This partnership of Church and Rogers continued until August 2, 1836 when it was dissolved and William opened a store of his own at 4 State Street. He occupied these premises for nearly twenty years.

The announcement stated, among other things, "J. Church has taken into the concern with him Mr. William Rogers, who has had experience in the different branches of the business." Also, "Silver spoons of the first quality will constantly be kept for sale and made to any particular pattern at short notice, and all other kinds of silver work."

Sometime prior to 1835, both brothers, Asa and Simeon, were working with William in the Church and Rogers store, but as early as 1830, Asa, also by now an accomplished spoon maker, formed a partnership with John A. Cole of Berlin, Connecticut and was advertising silver spoons in the *HARTFORD TIMES* of August 23, 1830. John Cole retired in 1832 and William became a partner. They advertised that, "The manufacture of SILVER SPOONS will be continued at the old stand."

This apparently was a restless period because this partnership, too, was dissolved by mutual consent on March 8, 1834 and Asa established "a Silver Spoon Manufactory" in Hartford "in the rear of the Post Office."

William continued in his shop on State Street making not only spoons but other gold and silver articles and selling a wide variety of jewelry, watches, etc.

Even in this early time William was apparently searching for any way to improve his silver products. In the *HARTFORD COURANT,* September 9, 1837 his advertisement mentions spoons and forks "made of pure sterling silver."

It may be surmised that he felt that the coin silver alloy was not the best for home use and experimented with the sterling

Coin Silver Spoons bearing original Rogers marks (1825–1860).

Coin Silver Spoons (reverse side). Left to right: Church & Rogers; Wm. Rogers; Rogers and Cole; (Eagle) Wm. Rogers (Star); A. Rogers, Jr. & Co.; (Eagle) Wm. Rogers & Co. (Star); (Eagle) Wm. Rogers & Son (Star).

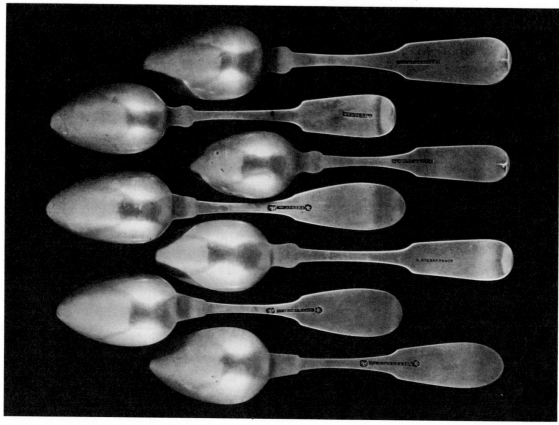

silver alloy. It's possible that he was one of the first, if not the first, to advertise the manufacturing and sale of sterling in this country.

During these early years, as some of the advertisements indicate, it was the general practice to use coins, American, Spanish, Mexican or English Crowns, generally obtaining them from those in circulation or from the banks, melt them into bars and roll and hammer them into spoons. That a very large amount of currency was absorbed by this practice, is proved by an article in the *HARTFORD COURANT* some one hundred and thirty-four years ago which says, "It is stated that ten thousand American or Mexican half-dollars are melted in Boston every week (about two hundred and fifty thousand dollars per year). New York and Philadelphia must use still more." There are also numerous records of complaints lodged in New York regarding the scarcity of silver change and it was recommended that banks issue bills for the fraction of a dollar.

Meanwhile, what about brother Simeon? Records show that he was working and learning his trade under William in the store on State Street and in 1841 was made a partner with the firm name changed to William Rogers and Company.

With this change of name the coin silver spoons they made were trademarked (Eagle) Wm. Rogers & Co. (Star).

The coming era of silverplate was to bring vast changes and enhanced reputation to the Rogers brothers and their long experience in the making of coin silver stood them in good stead.

Experiments in silverplating by electricity begin in this country around 1843 and both William and Asa were involved in them. They started manufacturing in a serious way in 1847 and in 1862 came with the Meriden Britannia Company to supervise the making of their product.

Wm. Rogers.

Asa H. Rogers.

Simeon Rogers.

163

Silver Plate Period

The year 1847 was an important one for the Rogers brothers, marking as it did for them the passing of the period of coin silver and the beginning of electro silverplate.

The way was not an easy one and the next twenty-five years were to see disagreements, financial difficulties and many partnership changes. But through it all they persisted in their determination to produce a superior product. Before long the Rogers quality was the one other makers sought to achieve.

John O. Mead of Philadelphia is usually credited with bringing to this country the first Smee galvanic battery which produced the electricity for silverplating by the new process patented by Elkington in England in 1840.

Among the experimenters in those early days and perhaps the very first to sell finished silverplated spoons in any quantity was Cowles and Company of Granby, Connecticut. (The area is shown as "Spoonville"

on old maps.) In 1843 Asa Rogers and James Isaacson joined them and by late 1844 plated ware was being made and sold in volume.

The following year, on November 13, the Cowles Manufacturing Company was formed by William B. Cowles, Asa Rogers (as secretary), James H. Isaacson and John D. Johnson. William Rogers gave financial assistance as evidenced by two recorded deeds, early in 1846, showing that all the land, water rights, buildings and equipment used by the Cowles Manufacturing Company on the Farmington River was deeded to William Rogers. A year later the other deed conveyed the property back to William B. Cowles.

From original account books preserved in the International Silver Company Historical Library we know that John O. Mead was working for Cowles Manufacturing Company late in 1845. From June 1846 to January 1847 a number of entries indicates he was paid two dollars a day and was paying board at the Cowles boarding house at five dollars and fifty cents a month.

William Rogers store at 4 State St. It was in the basement of this store that the Rogers brothers plated their first spoon in 1847.

Even while they were associated with Cowles in 1845 the Rogers brothers formed a partnership with Mead under the name of Rogers Brothers and Mead. This was short lived, however, and its dissolution was advertised in *THE HARTFORD TIMES* as of June 26, 1848.

William Rogers with brother, Simeon, had been selling Cowles plated spoons in his store from the beginning and in 1846 Asa left Cowles to join his brothers in Hartford. There in the basement of the store at 4 State Street they began producing their own silverplate in an important way.

This first silverplate was trademarked "Rogers Bros."

From the start, William insisted on maintaining rigid standards for quality. The finest grade of nickel (German) silver was used as a base metal. The mixture had to be right, the dies perfect and the metal of a shape and thickness to insure a durable product. All articles were weighed before and after plating to determine the amount of pure silver deposited and this had to conform to a predetermined scale of pennyweights and ounces per dozen pieces. The "Rogers Standard" became a guideline for the industry.

One of the first silverplated spoons made by the Rogers Brothers.

Probably the first printed price list for plated ware issued by Wm. Rogers in 1847.

W. ROGERS & CO.

SUPERIOR PLATED

SPOONS, FORKS, BUTTER KNIVES &C.,

No. 4, State Street,

HARTFORD, CONN.

PLATED ON FIRST QUALITY GERMAN SILVER.

Tea Spoons.			Dessert Spoons.			Table Spoons.			Forks.		
No.	Plain. Doz.	Tip'd. Doz.	No.	Plain. Doz.	Tip'd. Doz.	No.	Plain. Doz.	Tip'd. Doz.	No.	Dessert. Doz.	Table. Doz.
2	2 25	2 50	3	3 62½	4 00	4	5 00	5 50	4	7 50	8 00
3	2 75	3 00	4	4 25	4 62½	6	6 00	6 50	6	8 50	9 00
4	3 25	3 50	6	5 12½	5 50	8	7 00	7 50	8	9 50	10 00
6	4 25	4 50	9	6 62½	7 00	12	9 00	9 50	12	11 50	12 00

THREADED.

Soup Ladles.			Spoons.					Forks.		
No.	Plain. Ea	Thre'd Ea.	No	Table. Doz.	Dessert. Doz	Tea. Doz.		No	Table Doz.	Desert. Doz.
4	4 00	5 50	4	11 50	11 00	6 00		4	11 00	10 00
6	5 00	6 50	6	12 50	12 00	7 00		6	12 00	11 00
8	6 00	7 50	8	13 50	13 00	8 00		8	13 00	12 00
12	8 00	9 50	12	15 50	15 00	10 00		12	15 00	14 00

Butter Knives $6 00 per doz.

Other articles of Plated Work manufactured to order.

William was regarded as General Manager, being also head of the William Rogers and Company store, (Simeon was his partner), Asa, from his previous experience was doing the plating.

Even this early they were plating and selling not only spoons, forks, ladles, butter knives, etc. but also cake baskets, casters, tea sets, candlesticks and a host of other attractive articles for the home. They were steady advertisers in all three of the Hartford newspapers.

The business grew rapidly and soon required more space. In the fall of 1848 a move was made to an upper floor at 36 Pearl Street, corner of Trumbull Street, in what was known as the "Old Jail" building. This, too, proved inadequate and in 1853 a new company, Rogers Brothers Manufacturing Company, was formed. William was President and both he and Asa, large stockholders. Simeon became a stockholder a few months later.

They erected a four story, brick factory to suit their particular needs at the corner of Trumbull and Hicks Streets.

Early advertising of the new silver plate.

The old "Jail Building." It was to an upper floor in this building that the Rogers Brothers moved their business in 1848.

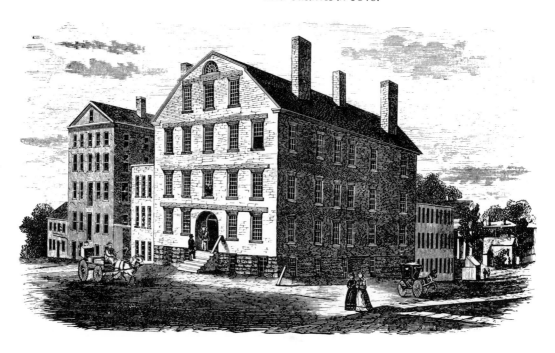

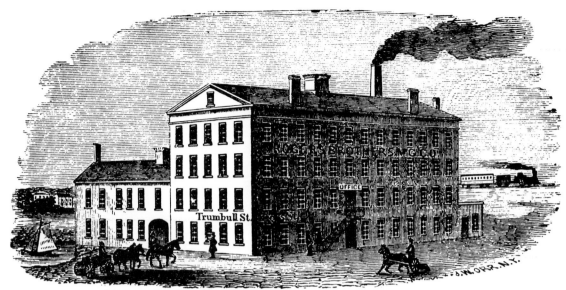

The new factory of Rogers Brothers Manufacturing Co., about 1853.

In 1856, for reasons not clear, William left the firm (although remaining as a director and stockholder) and with George W. Smith, a silverware maker of Albany, New York, organized Rogers, Smith and Company with William as President. The two firms were consolidated in the 1860's but continued to operate separate factories.

In 1862, like many other companies during and following the Civil War, they experienced financial trouble, with the pressure becoming so great they made an assignment to Meriden Britannia Company who bought the dies, tools, etc.

Meanwhile, in 1858, Asa and Simeon went to Waterbury, Connecticut and started a new business using the trademark (Star) Rogers and Bro.

In November of 1862 an agreement was made with Meriden Britannia Company for the three Rogers to come to Meriden to superintend the manufacturing of their famous silverplate. The trademark to be used was "1847 Rogers Bros." and this was the first year the numerals "1847" were used with "Rogers Bros."

A circular was issued to the trade stating that William, Asa and Simeon were located in West Meriden where their customers could, as formerly, "rely upon the superior quality" of goods they were manufacturing.

Rogers Smith & Co. about 1856.

*Photograph taken in front of the Meriden
Britannia Co. about 1873. Lower left is Asa Rogers
with scales. Card reads "Weighed in the balance and
found full weight." Asa H. Rogers*

The agreement did not require the entire time of the Rogers brothers and in 1865, William, because of some dispute, went to Hartford and formed William Rogers Manufacturing Company and taking into the business his son, William Rogers, Jr. The trademarks they used were "Wm. Rogers & Son," "Wm. Rogers Mfg. Co.," "1865 Wm. Rogers Mfg. Co." and "(Anchor) Rogers (Anchor)." Other members of the firm were Thomas Birch, William J. Pierce and William H. Watrous.

The agreement which William Rogers and his son made with the Meriden Britannia Company conflicted with one made with William Rogers Manufacturing Company and there followed a period of accusations, law suits, claims and counter claims too involved to detail here. In the end, Meriden Britannia on March 16, 1868 contracted to pay William and son five hundred dollars a month in advance for one hundred and twenty months beginning on March 20 of that year. (The two brothers, Asa and Simeon, had signed a fifteen year contract in 1862). These contracts were still in force when the three brothers died -- William in 1873, Simeon in 1874 and Asa in 1876.

William published an announcement in the NEW YORK MAIL of April 1, 1868 under the heading "Rogers Brothers Interests United" reading in part, "As all Rogers Stamps borrow their importance from the old Rogers Brothers reputation it has been deemed best to perpetuate this stamp as it is so thoroughly known throughout the country and from this time the old stamp of -- 1847 Rogers Brothers A1 -- will be used and guarded with all our digilance." Also, rather sadly, "I am getting to be an old man and viewing the matter on all sides have come to the con-

clusion that for me and the trade it is the best and wisest course."

The announcement ended with the words, "The quality is guarded by our honor and guarantee, and by a strong bond and our personal and constant supervision. Hoping for peace and a cessation from all troublesome elements, I remain William Rogers." He died five years later at the age of seventy-two.

When the contract expired in 1878 it was not renewed and William Rogers, Jr., the only survivor, went to Wallingford, Connecticut and made a long term contract with Simpson, Hall, Miller and Company to introduce a new brand of flatware bearing the trademark (Eagle) Wm. Rogers (Star). The mark had previously been used on coin silver but this was the first use on silverplated flatware.

These many companies associated with the Rogers brothers and the various trademarks used by them account for the confusion existing today among those interested in old silverware. In addition, there are other "Rogers" marks, not connected, but doubtless established to trade on the reputation established by the original Rogers brothers.

When International Silver Company was formed in 1898, William Rogers Manufacturing Company and related companies became part of it and it is still the only company making Original Rogers Silverplate.

The Rogers brothers did not invent the process of silverplating nor were they the first to do so in this country. However, there can be no doubt that they were the first to realize the commercial possibilities and to develop it so as to make possible, on a volume basis, the manufacturing and distribution of silverplated tableware in this country.

Meriden Flint Glass Co. about 1880–1882 showing glass furnace. This was built by Perkins and Lines, a forerunner of the present H. Wales Lines Co. with whose permission this photograph is used.

H. C. Wilcox, president of the Meriden Britannia Co. and leader in forming Meriden Flint Glass Co. He assumed the presidency of the latter concern when W. W. Lyman retired in 1883.

170

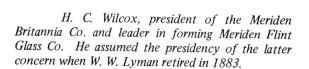

Joseph Bourne

For writers and historians, old journals, ships' logs and diaries have long been a rich source of information reflecting, as they do, the events and living conditions of the times they record.

No exception are two diaries, spanning the years 1877 and 1878 and 1880 and 1881, now preserved in the Historical Library of International Silver Company. They were faithfully kept by Joseph Bourne, superintendent of the Meriden Flint Glass Company and they furnish a wealth of information about the daily activity of the glass works as well as interesting things about Bourne himself.

The Meriden Flint Glass Company of Meriden, Connecticut was organized April 18, 1876 with Capital stock of fifty thousand dollars divided into two thousand shares at twenty-five dollars each.

The driving force behind the formation of this new enterprise was H. C. Wilcox, President of the Meriden Britannia Company since 1866. Fifteen hundred shares were held by the Meriden Britannia Company of which forty shares each were recorded in the names of H. C. Wilcox, I. C. Lewis, D. B. Hamilton, W. W. Lyman, L. J. Curtis, D. C. Wilcox and George R. Curtis to enable them to act as directors of the Flint Glass Company.

Two experienced glass makers from the New England Glass Works of East Cambridge, Massachusetts were promptly employed. They were George E. Hatch who was made Secretary and Sales Agent and Joseph Bourne, Superintendent. Each had forty shares of stock.

Originally a weekly Meriden newspaper reported that the New England Glass Works was about to move to Meriden but this rumor was soon set at rest by a complete report of the new company in the April 18, 1876 issue of the *MERIDEN DAILY REPUBLICAN:*

"The plans for the factory are now in the contractor's hands and work will be commenced at once. The building will be brick, two stories high, the main building to be two hundred and fifty feet by sixty feet. The cone for the glass works will be eighty feet high, twenty feet in diameter and sixty-seven feet in circumference."

On the eleventh of November, 1876, the fires were lighted -- "the office being performed by a young lady, the daughter of the president of the company." (W. W. Lyman)

The establishment of this new company was considered important enough for a New York newspaper to feature a lengthy article entitled "A Meriden Enterprise" in the issue of March 10, 1877. It stated, among other things:

"On the fourteenth day of December 1876, the work of manufacturing goods for market was practically begun. Since that date operations have gone forward without interruption.

...Under ordinary circumstances from one-third to one-half of the pots are broken during the process of heating up. So rare are the exceptions that men of long experience can give no instances of

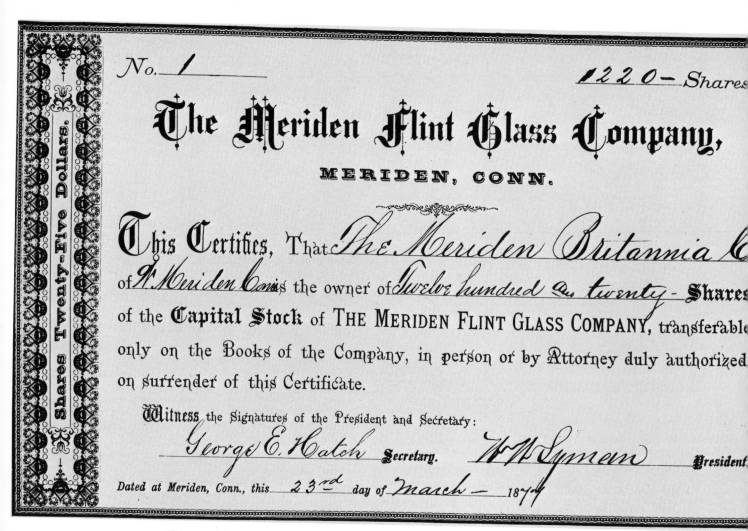

No. **1**   *1220* — Shares

The Meriden Flint Glass Company,

MERIDEN, CONN.

This Certifies, That *The Meriden Britannia Co.* of *W. Meriden Conn* is the owner of *Twelve hundred & twenty-* Shares of the **Capital Stock** of THE MERIDEN FLINT GLASS COMPANY, transferable only on the Books of the Company, in person or by Attorney duly authorized, on surrender of this Certificate.

Witness the Signatures of the President and Secretary:

George E. Hatch Secretary.   *W W Lyman* President.

Dated at Meriden, Conn., this **23rd** day of *March* — 187*4*

Shares Twenty-Five Dollars.

This was the simple stock certificate used by The Meriden Flint Glass Co.

Advertisement from Meriden City Directory of 1885.

furnaces heated up without breaking more or less. In this case not a single one was broken. Neither have any been broken during an active service of more than ten weeks."

An interesting account in the MERIDEN EVENING PRESS, January 3, 1882 describes in part the glass house or furnace room:

"It has ten arches at its base, each arch being ten feet high and containing a crucible of German clay in which the glass is melted, each crucible weighing a ton and holding 2500 pounds of metal (Material). It takes 2000 degrees of Fahrenheit to melt the metal and the capacity of the furnace is 50,000 pounds of metal a week. The sand used is imported from the Berkshire hills (Cheshire, Massachusetts) costing ten dollars a barrel delivered and is as pure and white as granulated sugar which it resembles."

The town of Meriden (Connecticut) as a site for a glass works would appear to be a very wise one. It was the center of the silver industry - the location of the Meriden Britannia Company (largest silver company in the world), Wilcox Silver Plate Company, Meriden Silver Plate Company, and in nearby Wallingford, Simpson, Hall, Miller and Company.

The Meriden Flint Glass Co. apparently had no trademark of its own but some of the glass they made for the Meriden Britannia Co. has that mark fired right into the glass.

These firms used tremendous amounts of glass for their silver pieces, including salts, peppers, mustards and cruets with glass stoppers for oil and vinegar, for the popular dinner casters. Also jars for pickle casters, linings for berry and preserve dishes, very fancy glass bowls for fruit baskets (now called brides baskets), vases, epergnes and other things too numerous to list.

The dinner caster was one of the most popular pieces in silverplate in the 1880's. They were made in great variety by all of the silver makers both in Meriden and elsewhere.

A rough idea of the popularity may be gained from this inventory of bottles in stock recorded by Bourne April 20, 1881.

(Style) No. 13

Vinegars - 2108 dozen
Peppers - 3114 dozen
Mustards - 1280 dozen

No. 11

Vinegars - 126 dozen
Peppers - 3195 dozen
Mustards - 1710 dozen

No. 2 1/2

Vinegars - 900 dozen
Peppers - 3131 dozen
Mustards - 3059 dozen

A grand total of 223,476 bottles of all kinds.

In addition in Meriden there were two lamp makers with worldwide distribution - the Bradley and Hubbard Manufacturing Company and Edward Miller and Company.

These firms made kerosene lamps with bases of glass as well as brass and nickel and also needed shades, globes and chimneys.

Cut glass was also very popular and besides other cut glass firms in Meriden both Meriden Silver Plate and Wilcox had large cut glass departments.

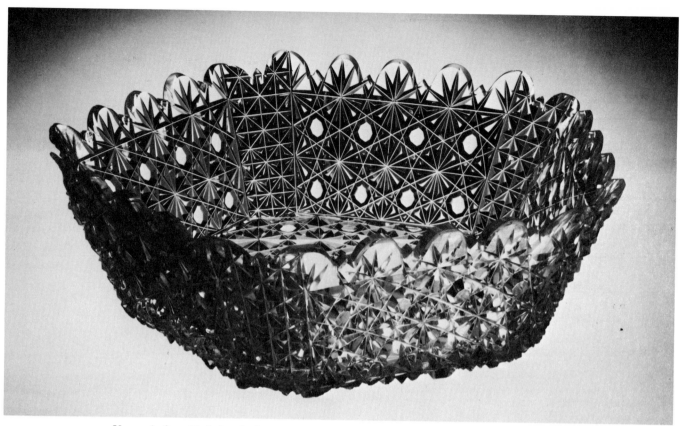

Unusual five-sided bowl, heavy cut glass. Made and cut by Meriden Flint Glass Co. All surfaces and cuts hand polished. Collection of Mollie Callahan Nolan.

Besides all this there was the market for sales from other parts of the country which could be drummed up by George Hatch and the other sales agents.

The Meriden Flint Glass Company made all these things and more besides.

But it is the diaries kept by Mr. Bourne which reveal the day by day operations and the trials and tribulations of running a glass works. Following are only a few of the entries in what he called his "Diary of matters connected with the Meriden (Flint) Glass Works - commencing January 1, 1877."

"January 1st - 7 pots of glass plain and good colour - white especially good - no pots broken - making 7 1/2 in. globes and No. 3 vases and vases with thread on top - also mustards & peppers. The engine not running owing to an unequal Ballance of the bank wheel of shaft of cutting shop - and other small deficiencies - sent for an expert from Hartford who understands the Corliss Engine."

"January 12 - Glass all right but furnace cold - poor coal - making vinegars, 14 inch shades coming out good - making clarets, chimneys, creams and odd work. Made 10 inch bowls today for rich cutting."

"January 22nd - commenced at 5 o'clock p.m. to burn coal to test how much we burn in one week - weighed one wheelbarrow full - 270 pounds."

"January 24th - one year today, by the date, since I gave my notice to quit the New England Glass Company. Paid the last installment of stock in the Meriden Flint Glass Company - two hundred and fifty dollars."

"February 2nd - gathered out a ball of clear glass No. 6 (Pot) the Best and clearest glass - also colour made yet - water colour."

"February 3rd - Painted shades all first rate - Mr. Wilcox delighted."

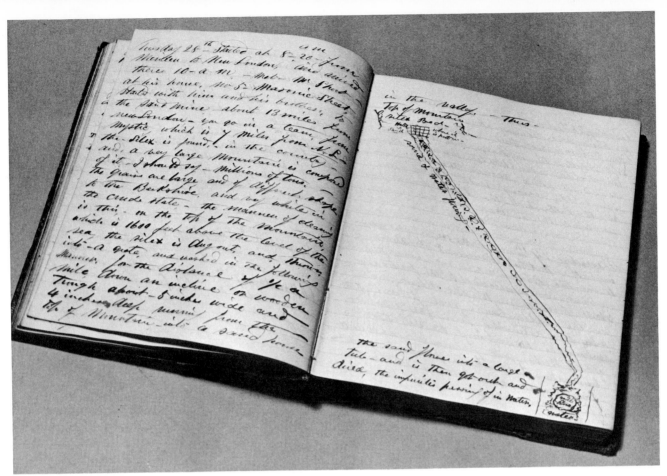

Bourne's diary entry describing his trip to a new sand mine and sketch showing method of washing the sand.

Typical entries from Joseph Bourne's diaries. "Wednesday 18th" he noted that the "Opal in No. 4 not good."

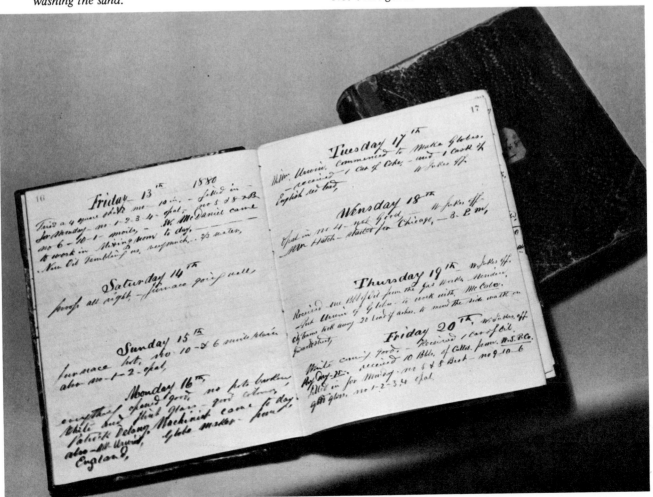

On February 5th, it was decided to build a certain wall in the glass house. Mr. Bourne described it with the added comment: "Commenced to dig out foundation about 10:00 a.m. - dug out a pit and when John Cady came to work he fell in and bruised his head and nose very much."

"February 14th - making tumblers, castor bottles and stoppers - 2 ring French shades - all the glass of a nice bright colour. Today a detective from Sandwich came and enquired for M. Montague and arrested him for having been concerned in a robbery at Sandwich of a clothing store."

"June 15th - goblets, champagnes, wines, custards and spoon holders coming out. Two agents of Boston and Sandwich Glass Company here today - were very favorably impressed with the Glass."

"July 18th - commenced making the founts (fonts) for Miller and Company."

"July 24th - the mobs of Philadelphia, Chicago, St. Louis, Pittsburgh still on the fighting and destroying path - all transportation West and South of New York suspended."

"August 6th - commenced on the small kiln today - the inside of kiln will be 7 feet long and 6 feet 11 inches wide."

"August 14 - my birthday - 51 years of age."

It is impractical in an account of this kind to quote all the entries in Mr. Bourne's diaries. He was responsible for the operation of the glass house, a twenty-four hour, seven days a week operation, the mixing of all the batches of different kinds of glass, the hiring and firing of help, the investigating of new sources of sand and different methods of heating furnaces (gas and oil) and was indefatigable in his pursuit of these duties.

On August 24, 1877 the shop was closed down for a week because of the extreme hot weather but Mr. Bourne did not take a vacation.

He records, on August 28, this detailed account of a lengthy trip:

"Started at 8:20 a.m. from Meriden to New London and arrived there 10:00 a.m. Met Mr. Short at his house No. 5 Masonic St. - started with him and his brother to sand mine about 13 miles from New London. You go in a team from Mystic which is 7 miles from New London. The Silex is found in the country and a very large mountain is composed of it - I should say millions of tons - the grains are large and a different shape to the Berkshire and very white in the crude state - the manner of cleaning is this - on the top of the mountain which is 1600 feet above the level of the sea the silex is dug out and thrown into a grate and washed in the following manner for the distance of 1/2 a mile down an incline on wooden trough about 5 inches wide and 4 inches deep running from the top of mountain into a sand house in the valley, the sand flows into a large tub - and is then got out and dried, the impurities passing off in water."

"Got some specimens of sand and returned to New London at 5 p.m. very tired - went up to Mr. Shorts to supper - met his mother and sisters who treated me very kindly and after going around the city spent the evening with them and, at 11 p.m., took the boat for New York arriving there at 7 a.m. (the 29th)."

On that day he visited glass houses in Brooklyn and at four p.m. took the New Haven boat, arrived there at ten p.m., and took the twelve o'clock car for Springfield and arrived at two a.m. Someone took his valise and he reports, "I had another with a whole set of dressing materials in it."

"September 7th set 2 pots No. 3 & 9 6 a.m. at glass house all day. Made some ruby lanterns (globes) for N.Y. & Fishkill R.R."

More were made on the 12th plus fourteen inch shades for Bradley and Hubbard. On October 1 "large order received from Mr. Boughton (agent) for rich cut goods" and on the 5th "lots of work."

An amusing incident is recorded on October 15 - "Mr. Clarke gave the men and boys some grapes for their good conduct in not stealing them." (Mr. Clarke's property was next to the glass works.)

"November 6th - making outside Blue Plated globes and ruby flashed on White Biscuit Jars."

"December 27 - quite a number of visitors here today. Making white goods and pickles (jars) for cutting also celeries."

"December 28 - making plated ware - ruby, green, blue on white. Made a very large vase 24 x 8.

"Monday, December 31 and last day of the year (1877) - It died surrounded by sunshine without the snow - a very beautiful day - glass opened good - all hands working. In the afternoon B. McCord came from Cambridge. Was much delighted with the place. Engaged him to come Monday - 7th day of January 1878 - wages $2.75 per move - T. Collins to serve him - his pay to be $2.00 per move. Making globes, shades, goblets, bottles, castor and heroes, chimneys and a variety of odd ware. A very beautiful day - this has been to me a year of sickness and great anxiety which rendered it a continual drag upon my system but today at the close of the year - I feel well and upon the whole the result of the year's labor has been fair - there seems to be a satisfaction generally that we have done well under the circumstances."

Right: Opal glass biscuit jar with lovely exterior of shaded pink and raised gold decoration of peacock and flowers. The silverplated lid and the base of the biscuit jar bear the Meriden Britannia Company's trademark illustrated on these pages; ca. 1880. Height 6¾". Left: Nut bowl of pressed optic patterned blue glass with colored Coralene decoration sets upon a silverplated stand made by the Wilcox Silver Plate Company. The blue glass bowl is attributed to the Meriden Flint Glass Company. Height 8". Collection Lionel V. DeRagon.

Copper-wheel engraved flint glass nappie. Made and decorated by Meriden Flint Glass Co. Rim originally gold colored. Collection of Mollie Callahan Nolan.

Nappie made and cut by Meriden Flint Glass Co. Collection of Mollie Callahan Nolan.

A Bizarre Invention

This fantastic idea shows up in three entries in Bourne's diary:

"October 18 (1877) - Mr. Teall here from Hartford to know about the possibility of making Glass Coffins."

"October 23rd - received a letter from Mr. Teall asking me to come to Hartford and speak a good word for his patent on coffins."

"October 26 - went up to Hartford and gave my opinion on Glass Coffins which was not very favourable to the party who had the patent."

Patent drawings for Joseph Bourne's "Hero Shade" dated April 3, 1877. The letter "A" on the patent drawings indicates the clear glass area of the Hero shade; "B" represents the white or opal glass area.

The Hero Shade

A product which was to prove a steady seller for the Meriden Flint Glass Company was called the "Hero" shade. A New York newspaper for March 10, 1877 stated: "The advantages of this chimney consist of a white or opal glass shade, with a clear glass chimney joined to the shade in the process of manufacture which admits of the reflection of the light by the shade through the clear glass at the bottom upon surrounding objects."

This same report credits the invention to "the genius and enterprise of Mr. G. E. Hatch" but it is quite clear from numerous entries in the diaries that the credit belongs to Bourne.

Moreover, patent 189,180 dated April 3, 1877 was granted to Joseph Bourne.

Experiments began February 20, 1877 and recorded.

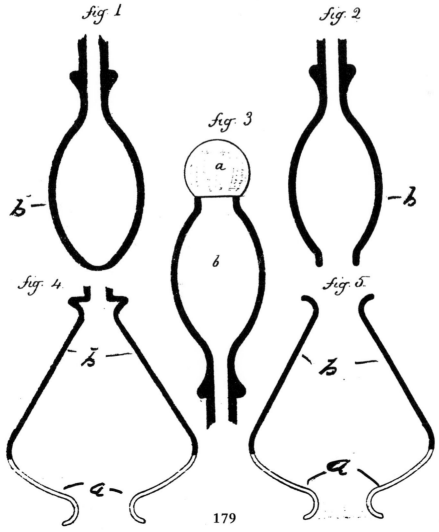

"Making a trial of shades - white and flint - to give a reflection of light downwards. Made today the first Hero shade by attaching the flint to the white by joining the two edges together."

"February 21st - the white and flint shade a success - under-part white, the other part flint will show light with either kerosene or gas and requires no chimney. Sold a large number to Stevens and Stocking at Cromwell (Conn.)."

"February 22nd - Mr. Wilcox and all parties much pleased with the shade - commenced to make a large number."

"March 7th - Directors meeting at the Glass Works. Mr. Lyman reported great excitement about the Hero shade."

"March 10 - Mr. Hatch sent a letter that he had an order for 1,000 dozen Hero Shades."

"March 24 - This afternoon I went and signed the patent for the mode of manufacturing the new Hero Shade and assigned it over to the Meriden Flint Glass Company - signed at Mr. Platt's office (lawyer) Palace Block."

On July 3, Bourne went to East Cambridge and "engaged T. Woods to make Heroes and J. Brooks to blow them."

On July 9, 10 and 11 - "making Heroes through the day - all hands."

April 21 (1878) agreed with Moore, McEthering and Company to make Heroes at the following price per dozen:

Gaffer	20 cents
Blower	16 cents
Put on flint	16 cents
Gatherer opal	8 cents
Gatherer flint	8 cents
Sticker up	6 cents
1st boy	4 cents
2nd boy	4 cents
LABOR	82 cents

He ends the year 1878 with this comment: "Last day of the year - started to Boston 9 a.m. Staid over at Springfield - in the evening went to Bowdin Square Church - watch night - very pleasant weather. Many people walking the streets at midnight, some making good wishes for the year - some drunk and others swearing - staid at Crawford House through the night."

Bourne's diaries continue all through 1880 and 1881 recording conditions at the Glass Works, what they were making, what pots broke, labor problems, receipts of supplies, rebuilding of the furnace, changes in the heating, trips taken to recruit glass workers, visits to other glass houses to view their products and methods, the weather, the state of his health, pay days, voting days, General Grant at Hartford, election of General Garfield as President of the United States November 2, 1880 (and his death September 18, 1881), a devastating tornado in Wallingford, Connecticut, and on September 1, 1880: "1st opening of the letter boxes and introduction of letter carriers. Name changed from "West Meriden' to 'Meriden."

An informative entry appears January 20, 1880: "Yearly meeting of Directors - report actual earnings $12,450 on $143,000 - same officers elected - at same salary."

Thermometer Tubes

Another product which proved to be of importance to the company was the drawing of glass tubing for use in thermometers, barometers and weather gauges.

The first indication of this appears on June 18, 1877 as - "White coming good - plating white for thermometer tube good - Mr. Kendal came this afternoon for thermometer tube."

On the following Tuesday they drew one hundred and thirty and one-half pounds, on Wednesday two hundred and fourteen pounds, and on Thursday one hundred and eighty pounds and nine pounds "red strip." Bourne figured the profit on this lot as one hundred and nine dollars and fourteen

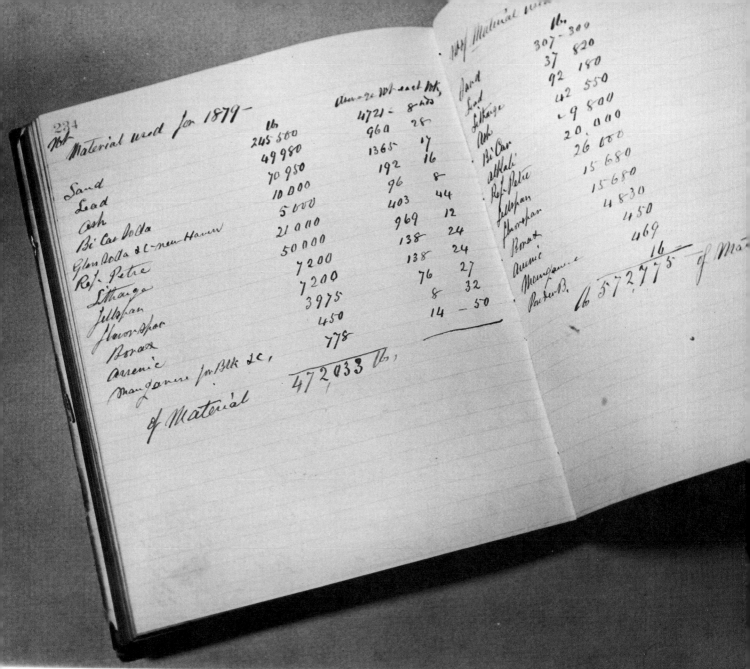

Bourne carefully recorded supplies used each year at the Meriden Flint Glass Company. These entries represent supplies purchased for the year 1879.

cents. "September 4, 1877 - Taylor from Rochester here for thermometer tube."

And on the 5th and 6th - "Making tube through the day." October 9, 10, 11 - making tube for Kendal. "Mr. Kendal having the ruby strip on tube also made some round small bore - he was much pleased at the lot he got in every way."

October 13 they were again drawing tube for Taylor and in four days drew one thousand, one hundred and forty pounds.

More was drawn for Kendal in November - seven hundred and thirteen pounds at a profit of one hundred and seventy-six dollars and ninety cents.

June 4—5, 1878 records drawing tube again for Kendal "10 men - 558 pounds - profit $136.72." And later in the month four hundred and ninety-five pounds for a Mr. Wilder.

All through the diaries there are similar notations periodically. It was evidently considered a profitable operation.

Intemperance

Intemperance may not have been a serious problem but it was prevalent enough to provoke such entries as these:

"January 9 (1877) - Stevens reported not fit for work from whiskey."

"January 16 - Stevens commenced after his sick drunken spell."

"October 29 - a disgraceful affair of drunkeness came to light today on the occasion of Cady's wife going to Portland. Moore, Wilkinson, Franklin, Jukes, King, McNaul, J. Collins and Cady. The result was in finally discharging King and W. Wilkinson."

"October 5 (1878) - Gave McEtheny a resolution to present to the G. M. (Glass Makers) Society. Resolved: that any member of this Society losing his time through intemperance shall be held responsible and pay the full value of the time any other member of the Society shall lose on his account - and the intemperate member shall also pay the full value of all unsalable goods made through his action of intemperance - the company for which he labors to receive the damages."

Bourne did not record whether or not this resolution was ever adopted. Maybe it helped but it did not stop the drinking. Only nine days later he notes - "Fogo in liquor - but at work."

Water Closets

It seems unlikely that a firm like Meriden Flint Glass Company making rich cut glass, flint glass stemware and fine colored glass of all kinds would consider making so mundane an object as a water closet. But they did.

Early in 1881 there are a few brief references to this and on May 9 - "Mr. Hatch notified that the patent for the water closet bowl was issued, also for the form of method of making it."

"June 1, 1881 - meeting on the water closet affair in Meriden B. Co. office."

"June 6 - commenced to make the water closets. McCabe made 40 - forenoon move. Bournequie in afternoon made 45 at 1/2 past 4 p.m."

"June 13 - commenced this morning to labor water closets out of kiln - 35 McCabe - Bourneique 42."

"June 16 - Bourneique's shop made 52 water closets in 4 hours."

McCabe made fifty-three more on the 23rd and they were again making them on the 29th and 30th.

The last reference is on August 17, 1881. Whether or not these were made on contract or on speculation is not known.

Another patent for glass water closet bowls, No. 286,000 was granted to George E. Hatch October 2, 1883 and assigned to the Hartford Sanitary Plumbing Company of Hartford, Connecticut.

In December of 1880 they were making blue crackled glass bottles, a new style castor bottle for Meriden Silver Plate Company and in 1881 the usual shades, canary and pea green toilet set bottles, black jewel boxes and ruby, green and amber plated ware among other things.

"January 1, 1881 - commenced to take stock, value of material in mixing room and Glass House - melting etc."

In colouring room - Amt. Stock	$4,267.50
In clay and pots - clay and pots	1,486.40
In coal - oil, etc. - fuel	2,527.34
	$8,281.24

An interesting entry appears: "March 24 (1881) - German here the name of Smith - E. Schmidt - Breslau, Germany with colours professing to put aniline colours of any kind upon glass and burn them in as perfect and clear as the mineral colours - through the agency of a Bindex - made from materials that will resist the "action of all acids on the strength of the chloride of lime - wanted fifty dollars for his secret."

In a statement at the end of the month, Mr. Bourne had this to say about it: "a fraud named Smith here to teach us how to colour with Aniline colours."

Joseph Bourne - The Man

It would be difficult to find a man more devoted to his work than Joseph Bourne. His home was quite close to the Glass Works and he was constantly alert to see that things were going properly regardless of the day or time.

Often, returning from a trip out of state he immediately went to the Glass House to check up. Or, for example - "Sunday, January 21 (1877) at the Glass House three times - everything going well."

Sometimes things didn't go so well, as on another Sunday - "February 4 (1877) in the evening - at 1/2 past 10 o'clock the opal pot - No. 4 - broke - ran out about 3 inches and ladled out the rest - here until after one a.m. Monday."

Or again on July 31, 1877 - "3 o'clock a.m. No. 7 opal commenced to run - worked it out - made 7 moves and found two small holes in the back just above the bottom. No. 10 also commenced to run about the same time - ladled it out. (This is the first time we have had two pots to break in one day.)"

He had a profound knowledge of glass making, not only in the mixing, coloring and melting but also in proper construction and ordered all the necessary brick, clay, etc.

His diaries are filled with notes on this phase of the business, complete with dimensions and often accompanied by sketches showing just what was done.

When something went wrong they sent for Mr. Bourne.

Early in August 1881, following a period of sickness he was in Boston for a brief vacation and records - "Returned home on receipt of telegraph August 12, 1881. Furnace had run down and heat could not be obtained to melt the glass."

Two days later - "furnace as hot as can be obtained with coal on hand," and on the following day he sent down to the Meriden Britannia Company for two loads of coal and reported "furnace commenced to recover."

"August 17 - furnace almost up to regular heat. All hands working on opal - making shades and water closets."

Bourne was knowledgeable enough to take full advantage of a chemical analysis service available through the state and on August 14, 1877 journied to New Haven with Mr. Lyman to see Professor Silliman, the state chemist. He brought samples for him to analyze.

The final report came through March 5, 1878. "Professor Silliman visited - final report on sand. Quality of the sand in nature was good but it was very badly washed and the foreign matter retained gave it poor qualities for making good glass. Manganese was impure. Not a marketable article for our purpose and had much iron in it."

"Sand sent sived (sieved) of Deans No. 1. Gave 99.49% of silica but washing poor. No. 2 taken from Gordon's sand sent from the Bbl. gave pure Silex."

Mr. Bourne was a kind man and often reports visits to hospitals to friends and relatives of the workers. He advanced money to one worker so that he could "visit his wife in Massachusetts."

On October 30, 1877 "started for New York with Mrs. Lutz (wife of a glass worker) to see the German Consul." And the following day - "went with Mrs. Lutz to see the consul - he advised her to write to the court house of her own town."

He was a sociable man, too, and apparently enjoyed lectures, sermons and special dinners.

183

One such dinner was given at the Westminster Hotel by the friends of George Wilcox, A. Bradshaw and Charles Monroe on going to Europe May 27, 1880. (George Wilcox was the son of H. C. Wilcox and later President of International Silver Company from 1907 to August 29, 1928. A. Bradshaw was a salesman for Meriden Britannia Company. Charles Monroe was a designer for the Meriden Flint Glass Company. He later went into business for himself and his company made the famous Wavecrest ware.)

On that occasion the following poem was read by John Blackburn but composed by J. Bourne.

"Goodbye, dear friends, a pleasant time
    We wish you on the rolling sea
And when you reach a foreign clime
    May fortune smile upon the three.
Adieu, we hope to meet again
    In the land you leave today
If not, our friendship will remain
    Though time may keep you far away.
You leave your home and native shore,
    And all the loving girls behind,
Whose friendship ever is in store,
    For those who treat them kind.
Then don't forget your home made vows.
    For foreign wealth or beauty.
But keep in mind mid all your days
    Your home, your love, your duty.
Farewell dear friends this little band
    Who meet tonight in friendship's bower
Will cheer you off, for the motherland
    In care of God's protecting power.
And may sweet memories of friends and home
    Keep hope and love in good repair
And bless you all, where-ere you roam
    With health - and lots of cash to spare."

(Later that year he wrote a lengthy poem on the occasion of the marriage of John Blackburn.)

Mr. Bourne seems never to have been in robust health and all through the four years of the diaries there are mentions of being sick with "chills" or the "shakes" or "malaria." Even so, it seldom kept him from his work.

Generally, the entries for 1881 are sparser and less detailed than previous years. He records much sickness during 1881 and notes on: "September 21st from today I remained home - very sick - and did not come to Glass House until Friday, the 11th day of November."

There are no entries for that long period. He ends the year 1881 prosaically with this entry: "Saturday 31st - Clear cold day - shops working in the forenoon - tinning the roof of shed - taking stock in the afternoon."

There is no diary for 1882 and Joseph Bourne died April 19 of that year.

Obituary

Death of Joseph Bourne

The many friends of Joseph Bourne will be pained to hear of his death, which occurred Wednesday night at about half past ten. He had not been in robust health for some years, and his last illness lasted about two months, although he was only for a few days considered dangerously ill. The immediate cause of his death was heart disease. He had been sitting up in bed, and had asked his wife to lay him down, but died while she was complying with his last request. Mr. Bourne had been superintendent of the Flint Glass Works ever since its formation, and was greatly beloved and respected by all its employees and officers as well as by his numerous friends. Mr. Bourne was a native of England and was fifty-six years of age. He leaves a wife and three daughters, Mrs. C. H. Lake of Boston, who formerly resided here, and Misses May and Emma. He was a member of the Knights of Honor and the Sons of Temperance. The funeral arrangements have not yet been completed, but the remains will be taken to Cambridge, Massachusetts for interment.

In 1883, W. W. Lyman, who had been president of the Glass Works from the beginning, retired from office. The position was then assumed by H. C. Wilcox.

George Hatch left in 1884 to go into business with T. B. Clark in Honesdale, Pa.

George R. Curtis, treasurer of the Meriden Britannia Company, was then elected secretary and treasurer.

Research has failed to disclose the exact reason why the Meriden Flint Glass Company went out of business and they are last listed in the Meriden City Directory for 1886.

A news item in the Meriden Daily Republican on September 28, 1887 states that "the Flint Glass Works suspended business two years ago."

The plant was then cleaned out and leased for two years to James J. Murray and Company who started making glass about August 15, 1887.

This continued to June 23, 1888 when the works were shut down for good. Many of the workers followed Murray to Philadelphia to a new shop he was building there and which expected to start operations August 15, 1888.

On October 9, 1885 the flint glass workers union had started a strike which closed virtually all the flint glass works in Pennsylvania, New York and New England. This may have been an influencing factor in the decision to suspend operations.

It may also be that following Joseph Bourne's death it was impossible to find a man competent to take his place. When one thinks of the numerous functions he performed and the many problems solved so efficiently this assumption seems not at all unreasonable.

Index

Extra plate, 98

F
Factory, Ashbil Griswold, 159
Ferris, G. W. Gale, 47
Ferris wheel, 47, 48
Food pushers, 103
Forbes Silver Co., 106, 142
Frary, James, 147, 151, 153
Frary, James S. and Co., 157
Frary, Roxanna G., 151
Fruit,
    bowls, 63, 119
    Jar, The Lyman, 158
    knives, 66
    stands, 119

G
Glass coffins, 179
Gorham Mfg. Co., 17
Granby, Conn., 164
Greenaway, Kate, 27
Griswold, Ashbil, 147
Griswold and Couch, 151, 155
Gudebrod, Louis, 21

H
Hamilton, D. B., 171
Harris, Elbridge, 158
Hartford,
    Courant, 161, 163
    Times, The, 165
Hatch, George E., 171, 174, 179,
    180, 182, 185
Hebbard, Alonzo, 37
Hero Fruit Jar Co., 158
Hero Shade, The, 179, 180
Herschfield, Henry, 18
Hiller, Louis C., 21
Holmes,
    and Edwards Silverplate, 107
    and Tuttle Mfg. Co., 98
Homer Laughlin China Co., 107
Homan Mfg. Co., 48

I
Ice pitchers, 35, 159
Infant feeding spoon, 102
Intemperance, 182
International Silver Co., 18, 21, 27,
    39, 59, 81, 84, 98, 101, 107,
    119, 123, 169, 171
Isaacson, James H., 164
Isabella Pattern, 98

J
Jewel caskets, 113
Johnson, John D., 164
Johnson, W. H., 156

L
Lavatory sets, 129
La Vigne Pattern, 98
Lewis, I. C., 151, 153, 155, 171

Linden Pattern, 90
Lyman, Andrew, 153
Lyman, Ann (Hall), 153
Lyman's Patent double valve, 37,
    159
Lyman, William W., 147, 151, 153,
    155, 156, 159, 171, 180, 183,
    185
Lyman, W. W. and Co., 156

M
Martineau, Harriet, 81
Match safes, 82
McCall, Betsy, 107
McCalls Magazine, 107
Mead, John O., 164
Meriden,
    Britannia Co., 11, 18, 20, 23,
        27, 35, 37, 43, 47, 48, 63,
        69, 70, 81–84, 95, 98, 101,
        104, 106, 111, 119, 123,
        129, 135, 142, 153, 155,
        156, 158, 159, 163, 167,
        169, 171, 173, 183, 185
    Bronze Co., 23
    Cutlery Co., 155
    Daily Republican, 171
    Evening Press, 173, 185
    Flint Glass Co., 47, 155, 159,
        171, 174, 179, 180, 184, 185
    Horse Railway Co., 155
    Silver Plate Co., 23, 27, 39, 48,
        81, 84, 111, 123, 142, 173,
        182
Mickey Mouse, 106
Middletown Plate Co., 23, 27, 38,
    59, 63, 111, 142
Miller and Co., Edward, 123, 173
Monroe, Charles, 184
Moselle Pattern, 98
Munson, John, 156
Murie, Margaret A., 109
Murray, James J. and Co., 185
Mustache cups, 90
My Own Set, 107

N
Napkin rings, 27
New England Glass Works, 171,
    174
New Haven and Fishkill R. R., 176
New York Mail, 169
Nut,
    bowls, 63
    cracks, 63
    picks, 66

O
Oddities, 81
Oil lamps, 123
Old Jail Building, 166
Oneida, Ltd., 98
Orange peelers, 92

188